The Asian Literature Bibliography Series

GUIDE TO JAPANESE POETRY

The Asian Literature Program
of the Asia Society

General Editor

Guide to

JAPANESE POETRY

J. THOMAS RIMER
AND
ROBERT E. MORRELL

G. K. HALL & CO.
70 LINCOLN STREET, BOSTON, MASS.
1975

Library of Congress Cataloging in Publication Data

Rimer, J. Thomas.
  Guide to Japanese poetry.

  (The Asian literature bibliography series)
  Includes index.
  1. Japanese poetry—Translations into English—
Bibliography. 2. English poetry—Translations from
Japanese—Bibliography. I. Morrell, Robert E., joint
author. II. Title. III. Series.
Z3308.L5R54   1975   016.8956′1′008   74-20610
ISBN 0-8161-1111-1

MANUFACTURED IN THE UNITED STATES OF AMERICA

to
Robert H. Brower
and
Donald Keene
with respect and affection

CONTENTS

FOREWORD

This annotated bibliography series on Asian literature was initiated in response to the needs of the nonspecialist. In each volume, a general introduction to the literature under examination precedes the annotations which provide summaries and evaluations to selected works. It is hoped that these guides will aid educators and students of Asian literature as well as those in disciplines other than literature—Asian heritage studies, anthropology, history, philosophy, the social sciences —who wish to take advantage of translated literature as a rich source of material for their studies. Books that are not available in libraries may be ordered through the publishers or through such specialized bookstores as Paragon Book Gallery, New York, Hutchins Oriental Books, California, or The Cellar Book Shop, Michigan.

Naturally, each author has his own criteria for the way the material in his guide is selected, presented, and judged. However, the intent of the author has been to indicate clearly and honestly the range and artistic merit of all the titles annotated and thereby guide the reader to those specific works that will satisfy his scholarly and aesthetic needs.

Arranged by topic and chronology, each guide covers the translated literature from the earliest times to today, but none pretend to be comprehensive. In most cases, works that are not recommended or have been superseded by better versions have been excluded. Omitted also are very specialized studies and inaccessible translations (thus excluding much of what has appeared in magazines and journals), and a number of translations too new to have been included in the guides. This increase in translation activities is a welcome sign. It points to a growing awareness of the importance of listening to Asian voices (rather than only to Western interpreters of Asia) and to the growing recognition of the place of Asian writings in world literature and of the place of translators in the creative field. Hopefully, these guides will serve the reader who later turns to translations not annotated or discussed here.

A series of this scope required the involvement of a number of people. I would especially like to thank the authors who have prepared these guides and the many scholars who have acted as consultants throughout the preparation of each manuscript, offering invaluable suggestions and criticism. Acknowledgment is also due Junnko Tozaki Haverlick of the Asian Literature Program of The Asia Society under whose editorial guidance these guides were prepared.

BONNIE R. CROWN, Director
The Asia Society   *Asian Literature Program*

NOTE TO THE READER

Pronunciation of Japanese. For our purposes, Donald Keene's brief guidelines will suffice. The consonants are pronounced as in English (with *g* always hard), the vowels as in Italian. Thus, the name Ise is pronounced "ee-say" (*Anthology of Japanese Literature*). For a more elaborate discussion, see "The Pronunciation of Chinese, Korean and Japanese" in Reischauer and Fairbank, *East Asia: The Great Tradition* (Boston: Houghton Mifflin Co., 1958 and 1960; Tokyo: Charles E. Tuttle Co., 1962), pp. 675-77.

Japanese Names. We follow the normal usage of listing the family name before the given name, except in citing book titles and quoting from the texts.

Bibliography. The annotated works within each literary period are organized topically where this is practicable and in order of their usefulness. Readers looking for a specific work are advised to check the index under author or title. Boldface numbers given for cross-reference refer to entry numbers, not page numbers.

ACKNOWLEDGMENTS

Every reasonable effort has been made to trace the owners of copyrighted materials in this book. The Asia Society apologizes for any omissions. For reprint permission grateful acknowledgment is made to:

Alfred A. Knopf, Inc. for Shakespearian verse from *Hamlet* in Japanese, tr. by George Sansom from *The Western World and Japan*, copyright © 1950 by George Sansom.

Carcanet Press Ltd. for "In a stony place..." and "Day of Metamorphosis" by Takagi Kyōzō, tr. by James Kirkup and Nakano Michio from *Selected Poems*, copyright © 1973 by James Kirkup and Nakano Michio.

Charles E. Tuttle Co. for "The swimmer's body stretches out slanting..." by Hagiwara Sakutarō, tr. by Edith Shiffert and Sawa Yūki from *Anthology of Modern Japanese Poetry*, copyright © 1972 by Charles E. Tuttle Co.

Chicago Review for "My sufferings are simple..." by Tamura Ryūichi, tr. by Sato Hiroaki from *Anthology of Modern Japanese Poets* (vol. 25, no. 2, 1973), copyright © 1973 by *Chicago Review*.

Chicago Review Press for "The gray light avalanched..." by Miyazawa Kenji, tr. by Sato Hiroaki from *Spring & Asura*, copyright © 1973 by Chicago Review Press.

Doubleday & Company, Inc. for "Won't you come and see..." by Matsuo Bashō, tr. by Harold G. Henderson from *An Introduction to Haiku*, copyright © 1958 by Harold G. Henderson; four lines from a poem by Takahashi Shinkichi, tr. by Lucien Stryk and Takashi Ikemoto from *Afterimages: Zen Poems*, copyright © 1972 by Lucien Stryk and Takashi Ikemoto.

George Allen & Unwin Ltd. for "Many clouds arise..." tr. by W. G. Aston from *Nihongi*, copyright © 1956 by George Allen & Unwin Ltd.

Granite Publications for "The swimmer's body expands

Kodansha International Ltd. for "Wife and mother..." tr. by Eric Sackheim from *The Silent Firefly*, copyright © 1963 by Kodansha International Ltd.

Kyoto Seika Junior College Press for "How can I tell the floating world..." and "What can I compare/ The world to..." by Ryōkan, tr. by Kodama Misao and Yanagishima Hikosaku from *Ryōkan the Great Fool*.

Monograph Committee for "It's love, they all say..." by Mibu no Tadamine, tr. by Grant Sharman from *One Hundred Poets*, copyright © 1965 by Grant Sharman.

Mushinsha/ Grossman Publishers Inc. for "As long as I have life..." by Ho-wori-no-mikoto, tr. by Donald Philippi from *This Wine of Peace, This Wine of Laughter*, copyright © 1968 by Mushinsha Ltd.; *haiku* by Matsuo Bashō, tr. by Cid Corman from *Back Roads to Far Towns*, copyright © 1968 by Cid Corman; "along this route..." by Matsuo Bashō, tr. by Maeda Cana from *Monkey's Raincoat*; "The Earthquake" by Kokan Shiren, tr. by Marian Ury from *Poems of the Five Mountains*.

New Directions Publishing Corp. for "I passed by the beach..." by Yamabe No Akahito, tr. by Kenneth Rexroth from *One Hundred Poems from the Japanese*. All rights reserved. Reprinted by permission of New Directions Publishing Corporation.

Paragon Book Reprint Corp. for "Many clouds arise..." tr. by W. G. Aston from *Nihongi*, copyright © 1956 by George Allen & Unwin Ltd.

Penguin Books Ltd. for "Far-off Land" by Tamura Ryūichi, tr. by Geoffrey Bownas from *New Writing in Japan*, ed. by Geoffrey Bownas and Mishima Yukio, copyright © 1972 by Geoffrey Bownas and Mishima Yukio; "On a bare branch..." by Matsuo Bashō, and "The world of dew..." by Kobayashi Issa, tr. by Geoffrey Bownas and Anthony Thwaite from *The Penguin Book of Japanese Verse*, copyright © 1964 by Geoffrey Bownas and Anthony Thwaite; "A Far Country" by Tamura Ryūichi, tr. by Harry Guest, Lynn Guest and Kajima Shōzō from *Post-War Japanese Poetry*, copyright © 1972 by Harry Guest, Lynn Guest and Kajima Shōzō.

Purdue University Studies for "Incense smoke..." and "So that

University of Tokyo Press for "The many-fenced palace of IDUMO . . ." tr. by Donald L. Philippi from *Kojiki*, copyright © 1968 by University of Tokyo Press.

The University Press of Hawaii for "Rain in spring . . ." and "Look! Already I carry/ My hands . . ." by Ōkuma Kotomichi, tr. by Uyehara Yukuo and Marjorie Sinclair from *A Grass Path: Selected Poems from the "Sokeishū,"* copyright © 1955 by University of Hawaii Press.

Harold Wright for "Denying my heart . . ." by Saigyō, from "The Poetry of Japan" in *Asia* 16 (1969). Reprinted by permission of The Asia Society.

We wish to express our appreciation to The Asia Society, through its representative Bonnie R. Crown, for inviting us to prepare this guide; to Junnko T. Haverlick of The Asia Society, whose suggestions and attention to detail in developing the manuscript were invaluable; and to Washington University, for providing us with time and resources to complete the project.

One real pleasure we found in assembling this bibliography was to see the generally high quality of the books we included, and we share the same enthusiasm of many writers anxious to express their own attraction to this remarkable genre of Japanese literature. If this small book helps put the reader in touch with those enthusiasms, our labors will be richly repaid.

J.T.R.
R.M.

Washington University,
St. Louis

PART ONE:
GENERAL INTRODUCTION

GENERAL INTRODUCTION

Europe and the United States became aware of Japanese poetry less than a hundred years ago, when the first tentative translations by curious Westerners and enthusiastic Japanese were made available. Since that time, Japanese poetry has had considerable artistic impact on Western poetry and has won a place for itself both among general readers and with specialists of Japanese literature and culture, a fact to which the number of books and articles in this bibliography attest.

If early apprehensions of Japanese poetry were filtered through Victorian sensibilities of Americans and Europeans whose idea of poetry came from the reading of Longfellow, Tennyson, Hugo, and Heine, the evolution of poetry in our century, from Pound to Ferlinghetti, has prepared our sensibilities to understand better the nature of the particular poetic truth that the various manifestations of Japanese poetry possess.

Nevertheless, there are still barriers: the brevity of the poems, the repetition of similar images, and the treacherous problems of flat or clumsy translation. An informed reader can overcome these difficulties, of course, and it is our hope that this bibliography will give him the sources of information to help him do so.

Those who have read Japanese poetry are immediately struck by the fact that most of the poems are very brief. The poems are measured in syllables, not in lines as in Western poetry. For example, *waka* (alternately known as *tanka*), the dominant aristocratic verse form since the beginning of the poetic tradition, has only thirty-one syllables. If the sonnet can be taken as the standard form of the short poem in the Anglo-American tradition, we would not get much of Wordsworth; thirty-one syllables of the sonnet "Composed upon Westminister Bridge" would only permit:

> Earth has not anything to show more fair:
> Dull would he be of soul who could pass by
> A sight so touching in its majesty:
> This

13

Hardly a poem by any standard. The accomplishments of the *waka* poets seem all the more extraordinary, considering the limited poetic space in which they have to maneuver.

Sabishisa wa	Loneliness does not
sono iro to shi mo	Originate in any one
nakarikeri	Particular thing:
maki tatsu yama no	Evening in autumn over
aki no yūgure	The black pines of the mountain.

[Jakuren; tr. by Donald Keene,
Anthology of Japanese Literature, p. 195]

Even those not familiar with Japanese aesthetics will surely be able to sense in these words the eternal moving dialectic between the emotions of the poet and the sights that inspire his feelings.

Although the *waka* is short, the *haiku*, which has earned a certain following among American poets who write them in English, is even shorter, a mere seventeen syllables in all. Yet the man who many feel is the greatest of all Japanese poets, Matsuo Bashō (1644–94), was a *haiku* poet. His verse,

Furuike ya	The old pond;
kawazu tobikomu	A frog jumps in—
mizu no oto	The sound of water.

[Tr. by R.H. Blyth, *Haiku*, vol. 1, p. 277]

is known to every Japanese schoolchild and to increasing numbers of American ones as well.

Brevity does not mean simplicity, and numerous essays have been written on the meaning of this one poem. (After all, what is the essence of the *sound* of water?) Obviously a great deal can be accomplished in a *haiku*.

What is the reason for the brevity? A number of explanations are provided by scholars, and a certain number of these suggest important facts about the general nature of Japanese poetry. The first concerns the regularity of the sound patterns of the Japanese language. Japanese lacks many of the devices common to poetry written in Indo-European languages. There is no rhyme—or, rather, since almost everything has rhyme, it is to be avoided as an artistic technique. There are no consonant clusters, and no clear metrical devices (other than syllable count) to permit an interesting scansion line after line. Thus the prosody of a long poem risks a certain monotony for the eye and ear, and the language lends itself better to short forms. Secondly, the ambiguity of the Japanese language allows double meanings, puns on words, and a suggestive vagueness permitting a variety of overtones; number and gender are usually indeterminate or inferred from contexts, and subjects of sentences and phrases can normally be omitted. Such linguistic characteristics permit compactness of form without sacrificing fullness of meaning, and these have been exploited to the fullest by *waka* and *haiku* poets. The limitations of brevity are overcome and the reader, thrust into immediate contact with the images, participates in the poem and has perhaps a more direct artistic experience than may be possible with Western poetry, where the personality of the poet often interjects itself between the material of the poem and the reader's sensibilities.

Take, for example, some additional lines from the sonnet by Wordsworth.

> Never did the sun more beautifully steep
> In his first splendor, valley, rock, or hill;
> Ne'er saw I, never felt, a calm so deep!

Here is a *haiku* by Kobayashi Issa (1763–1827):

Assari to	Spring has come
haru wa kinikeri	In all its simplicity:
asagi-zora	A light yellow sky.

[Tr. by R.H. Blyth, *Haiku*, vol. 2, p. 38]

All the details stated by Wordsworth are in the *haiku* concentrated in the single image of the thin color of the sky. At least in the poem itself, the poet who says "ne'er saw I" is missing completely. Issa has selected the image of the sky and the conception of spring and juxtaposed them so that one epitomizes the other. The effect of both poems is profound, and as satisfying in the Issa as in the Wordsworth. Each poet understands the best possibilities of his own language.

Japanese poetry has not always been short. The first great collection of poetry written in Japanese, the *Manyōshū* (Collection for Ten Thousand Generations), compiled in the late eighth century, has a number of long poems (*chōka*), and those by Hitomaro are among the greatest in the language. Succeeding imperial anthologies chose to preserve the *waka* form almost exclusively. *Waka* and *haiku* remained the major forms until translations of Western poetry into Japanese in the late nineteenth century quickly convinced certain Japanese writers that the old forms, with their fixed subject matter and vocabulary, were no longer suitable for the treatment of important emotional and intellectual experiences. Various experiments were made to reproduce Western poetry in the traditional vocabulary, and some poems were written by Japanese poets in tentative imitation of Western models. But the translation, early in this century, of poems by the French Symbolists—Verlaine, Baudelaire, and others—showed the Japanese poets that means other than merely linguistic ones (rhyme, meter, etc.) were available to them for the organization of long poems. This new freedom permitted the creation of a considerable body of accomplished, often provocative, modern poetry in a free style, some of which is now available in translation.

While the progressive shortening of the basic poetic unit of traditional verse—from *chōka*, to *tanka*, to *haiku*—can partly be explained by reference to linguistic and aesthetic peculiarities, we should also note that the shortening was accompanied by procedures for organizing these basic units into larger complexes. It might be argued, indeed, that the long poetic statement did not really disappear but rather manifested itself through a variety of new guises: in the poetry contest (*utaawase*), in the later imperial anthologies and poetic sequences where *waka* were not simply grouped together at random but were consciously integrated, and in linked-verse (*renga*) composition which resulted in one large poem instead of a set of small discrete ones. The long poetic statement also can be found in fusions of poetry and prose in the poem-tales (*utamonogatari*), personal "diaries" (*nikki*), and travel diaries (*kikō*), which so merge together that we ask ourselves if these works are narratives embellished with verse, or poetry collections with elaborate prose annotations.

In 730, a Plum-blossom Viewing Banquet was held at the residence of the *Manyōshū* poet, Ōtomo Tabito, at which a set of six *waka* was composed by Tabito and his guests. Subsequently, the poetry contest became a major pastime of the Heian court, and the group composition of verse sequences was carried forward by the linked-verse movement from the Kamakura–Ashikaga period to modern times. Moreover, in the later imperial anthologies (e.g., the *Shinkokinshū*) and other contemporary collections, we find that *waka* by different persons were systematically selected and arranged by the compilers into coherent sequences—or, if you will, into long poems. And finally, in the poem-tales (*Ise monogatari, Yamato monogatari*, etc.) and in the personal and travel diaries of Ki no Tsurayuki, Izumi Shikibu, the nun Abutsu, Bashō, and Shiki, the prose is often little more than an extension of the poetry. Bashō was the great master of this technique, and his travel diaries, in which he mixed *haiku* with highly-wrought prose passages, often of a philosophical nature, represent a high point in Japanese literature. Yet in the earliest poetic diary we find this same fusion. In a passage from the *Tosa nikki* (935), Tsurayuki, having told us that the ship on which he had been traveling was holed up in Ōminato harbor and that the moon sinking into the sea had brought to mind a verse by Narihira, gives us this poem:

> As I look on the moon
> Shining in its flowing across the sky,
>   I see that the port-mouth
> Where the starry River of Heaven flows
> Is, like that of other streams, the sea.
> [Tr. by Earl Miner, *Japanese Poetic Diaries*, p. 66]

In short, we seem to have another instance of the principle that for every action there is an equal and opposite reaction, although Newton certainly did not have Japanese poetry in mind when he came upon the notion. The shortening of the basic unit of poetry was compensated for by the integration of short units into longer forms.

In all societies, no matter how the fact may be disguised, the composition of poetry of any conscious artistic nature is an aristocratic art, requiring learning, leisure, and sensitivity. In particular, traditional Japanese poetry in the earlier periods was a product of court circles. In the Tokugawa period (1600–1868), rule by military government brought stability after a long period of civil war, and the development of commerce in the cities produced a flourishing middle class in Japan's urban areas. Money and leisure brought a desire for culture, and poetry became somewhat democratized with the development of the *haiku*, considered a more accessible form of poetry for those not trained in the more rigorous traditions of *waka* poetry. As Bashō wrote, willow trees probably belonged in *waka*, but mud snails were fine for *haiku*. As a result, new vitality and new powers of observation produced a perhaps less profound, but a sharper and more observant, and on occasion, a more humorous poetry than *waka*. *Haiku* provide a clear-eyed view of the human condition and a genuine feeling for the mysteries of nature. Modern poetry, of course, has increased considerably the spectrum of possible subjects and emotional states feasible in Japanese, but it is not surprising that *waka* and *haiku* continue in their popularity and are written today for a large audience of fellow poets and readers.

Sometimes the contrary pull of different traditions is a source of apprehension. The words written by Kunikida Doppo (1871–1908), a fine novelist sensitive to his own culture, seem to mirror a psychology still recognizable by those who have read any significant amount of modern Japanese poetry:

... in my bosom, two different ideas are fighting for mastery: one is Eastern, what I have inherited; the other is Western, what I have received through my later education. I feel myself exaulted when I recite Wordsworth facing the morning rainbow, but what can I do when the curfew brings with it those unspeakable moving lines, those tanka of bygone days? ... [From Kōno Ichiro and Fukuda Rikutaro, *An Anthology of Modern Japanese Poetry*, p. xxi]

The tension between the Japanese sensibility and imported ideas has always been a source of great artistic creativity. China served as a catalyst in earlier times; the West serves the same function in our own century. Also, a creative tension exists between the individual and the social sensibility in which he participates. The aristocrats who had the time to read and study learned the older collections and based their new poems on the precedents they found there, even to the extent of reproducing a third of an older poem in their new one. Such a generous use of allusion may suggest a classicism, a closed world, even sterility. Yet for these poets, allusion was a satisfying means to enlarge the poet's world by conjuring up the world of another poem to add to, or to contrast, with his own. The poets knew that their allusions would be recognized, just as a contemporary Japanese poet can mention "The Wasteland" and know that he will be understood.

An English-speaking reader new to Japanese poetry will not make these connections, of course, but a little experience will permit him the pleasures of recognition as he sees the same themes, the same words, even the same concrete impressions changed and transmuted from poet to poet. The tradition of Japanese poetry seems to suggest an inexhaustible depth both in the world of nature and in the human emotional response to it. However learned the *waka* poets may have been, they never lost their understanding of the necessity for direct observation as a basis for their art.

What of the world of ideas? This dimension of poetry is of great importance in the history of Western art, from Dante and Milton, through Auden, Eliot, and Wallace Stevens. Moral and intellectual sensibility seem part of our comprehension of what poetry is. Some poems in the early *Manyōshū* are intellectual, even philosophical, in the treatment of their subject matter, and modern Japanese poetry is as rigorously analytical as any written in the West. *Waka* and *haiku* seem to be something else, however; we know how the poet *feels* but only by inference at best do we know how, or what, he *thinks*. There are reasons for this too. The court poets from early times wrote in Chinese as well as in Japanese. Classical Chinese served a number of countries in the Far East (Korea, Vietnam, Japan) in somewhat the same fashion that Latin did for medieval Europe: a common means of communication and a touchstone of linguistic taste. It also provided poetic vehicles for the sustained philosophical statement, while the shorter Japanese forms were reserved to evoke the immediacy of momentary sensuous experience. Early poems by the court nobility, verse by medieval Zen monks, and poetry by Tokugawa Confucian scholars are gradually beginning to engage the attention of Western translators.

Direct response remains the best way for the Western reader to appreciate Japanese poetry. The more cultivated the reader, the more discriminating will be his spontaneous response, and there are now a variety of materials available in English to help. One can, of course, read Japanese poetry for its religious dimensions, sensuous pleasure, unusual visual observations, and the

bitter-sweet complexities that result from the delights and futili-
ties of the human condition. Modern poetry even permits an
examination of the political and ideological position of the
writer. Basically, however, direct perception on the part of the
reader is the surest means to penetrate the poet's vision and
make it momentarily one's own—a direct perception brought
about by a few deft words so that they do not intrude between
the reader and the experience.

One problem with the brevity of Japanese poems is that one
may read them too quickly and penetrate superficially, perhaps
not at all. Mr. Yasuda points out in his stimulating book, *The
Japanese Haiku*, that the best poems are perfect and cannot be
altered. Take, for example, the celebrated *haiku* by Bashō:

Kare eda ni	On a bare branch
karasu no tomitari ya	A rook roosts:
aki no kure	Autumn dusk.

> [Tr. by Geoffrey Bownas and Anthony Thwaite,
> *The Penguin Book of Japanese Verse,* p. 111]

Change "rook" to "rooster" and the whole sense of the poem
is changed, shattered: all those bright feathers and the autumn
dusk has lost its gloom.

Another question a reader beginning to study Japanese poetry
will surely ask is, who are the great poets? The names are simple
to provide, but their work cannot be read in the fashion one
might read a Western poet. In Japan, most of the great *waka*
poetry, for example, was made available in anthologies compiled
under numerous editors and at various times. Works by the
great poet Saigyō (1118–90) are scattered in a dozen places and,
in any case, were not composed to be read consecutively. Many
of the linked-verse sequences were composed by several poets
at once, so that poems by any one author can scarcely be
separated out at all.

In order to be as helpful as possible with such problems,
we have provided, in the second part of this introduction, an
outline of the history of Japanese poetry—its forms, the major
books on poetry and criticism, and representative authors. Such
a brief account will hopefully give the reader a general sense
of the flow and development of this remarkable poetic tradition.
Following the narrative account of each period is a bibliographic
outline.

PART TWO:
HISTORICAL SKETCH AND
BIBLIOGRAPHIC OUTLINE

HISTORICAL SKETCH AND BIBLIOGRAPHIC OUTLINE

I. General Background and Introductory Surveys

The first step in organizing the materials of Japanese poetry is to place them in the context of world literature. Compared to a few traditions, the history of Japanese poetry is brief; compared to most, it is respectably long. Homer (ca. 800 B.C.), who is thought to have forged his epics from oral sources already several centuries old, stands at the beginning of the tradition of Greek poetry which continues to the present day. The Chinese *Book of Songs (Shih Ching,* ca. 600 B.C.), some parts of which may antedate the compilation by some four centuries, is the first great collection of poetry in a literary continuum whose latest representatives include Mao Tse-tung. Before these we find the Sumerian *Epic of Gilgamesh*, portions of which survive from the first half of the second millenium B.C., as well as the poetry of the Egyptians and other ancient peoples; but ancient Egyptian and Sumerian are no longer the media of living traditions.

Against this background, the *Collection for Ten Thousand Generations (Manyōshū)*, the first great collection of Japanese verse, is a rather recent arrival, being compiled around A.D. 759. (Although the *Manyōshū* and several works composed a few decades earlier contain material already a few centuries old, even the earliest poems are thought to have originated not prior to the fourth century.) Against a more familiar background, however, the *Manyōshū* appears ancient enough. The history of the English language can be conveniently divided into three periods, each of four hundred years duration. The first period is Old English (700–1100), whose outstanding literary work is the epic poem *Beowulf*, composed about 700. And Old English is far enough removed from the modern language as almost to be another tongue. Certainly a Japanese today has less difficulty reading the *Manyōshū* than we have deciphering *Beowulf* —assuming, of course, that he is not faced with the primitive transcription *(manyōgana)* in which the collection was originally recorded. While Murasaki Shikibu was writing the classic *Tale of Genji* (ca. 1000), Old English was still the medium of English literary expression (supplemented by Latin), and Harold had not yet met William the Conquerer at Hastings.

Middle English (1100–1500) absorbed the Norman influence, and in the latter part of the period, produced its representative work, the *Canterbury Tales*. In Japan, meanwhile, appeared a collection of verse second in importance only to the *Manyōshū*, the *New Collection of Ancient and Modern Times* (*Shinkokinshū*, 1206). The *Tale of the Heike* (*Heike monogatari*) took shape sometime between 1185 and 1220; and the fourteenth century saw the development of the *nō* theater with Kannami and his son Zeami.

Modern English (1500–1900+) begins with Spenser and Shakespeare and continues to the present day. In Japan, Sōgi, the master of linked-verse *(renga)* died in 1502; and the end of the following century witnessed the flowering of the merchant culture known as the Genroku period, with the poet Bashō, the novelist Saikaku, and the playwright Chikamatsu. In England, Bunyan was writing *The Pilgrim's Progress* (1678), Defoe, *Robinson Crusoe* (1719; first Japanese translation in 1859), and Swift, *Gulliver's Travels* (1726; Japanese translation in the Edo period).

In drawing attention to parallel or merely contemporaneous literary phenomena in Japan and the English-speaking world, we do not mean to imply that the two traditions had similar developments. If the juxtaposition seems curious or thought-provoking, our purpose is served. As we come to see Japan in the context of world literature, we must also become accustomed to seeing her in the context of world history. Is it not interesting to consider that Johann Sebastian Bach and the Zen reformer and calligrapher, Hakuin Zenji, were both born in 1685? In the words of the Roman playwright Terence, "I am a man, and I consider nothing human alien to me." He might have added: "—be it English or Japanese."

England and Japan are both island countries in the temperate zone, and both developed in the cultural shadow of earlier and impressive continental traditions, Rome and China respectively. Just as Chinese continued to be employed in Japan by many scholars long after an adequate writing system was developed to transcribe the Japanese tongue, so Latin persisted as the language of learning in England and the rest of Europe. Japan's cultural debt to China is well known to the West, but is easily exaggerated. It may help us to arrive at a more balanced appraisal of the phenomenon by considering the many cultural borrowings of our own forebears in the English-speaking tradition, including the prevalent use of Latin until modern times. Bede the Venerable's *Historia Ecclesiastica Gentis Anglorum* (completed in 731) has its counterpart in the *Chronicles of Japan* (*Nihon shoki*, 720), composed in Chinese. But from *Beowulf* until *Piers Plowman* and *The Canterbury Tales* in the fourteenth century, English literature has little to compare with the sudden flowering of Japanese letters which culminated in the *Tale of Genji* (ca. 1000) and continued to flourish fitfully for the next several centuries. During this same period the use of Latin, both written and spoken was common in England. We should not be surprised at the continued use of written Chinese by the Confucian scholars and historians of Tokugawa Japan (1600–1868) when we consider that well into modern times a number of the most significant works by "English" writers first appeared in Latin. These works include Thomas More's *Utopia* (1516), Francis Bacon's *Novum Organum* (1620), Newton's *Principia* (1687), and works by Thomas Hobbes. (*Leviathan*, however, appeared first in English, in 1651; a later version was published in Latin in 1668.)

Earlier in the introduction the general characteristics of Japanese poetry were discussed. In the following sections we will provide a sketch of the surprisingly varied developments within the tradition, relating them, where possible, to events in Western history. We begin with the periodization proposed by Brower and Miner in *Japanese Court Poetry* and continue with the familiar political periods from the military regimes of Kamakura and Ashikaga. Each descriptive section concludes with a bibliographic outline to call the reader's attention to specific topics covered in the books annotated in Part Three of this guide. These books will be grouped as consistently as possible according to the periodization employed in the introductory sketch, and we hope that the reader will join us in blaming the hobgoblin when he feels that a book has been misplaced.

Before proceeding with the chronological outline we wish to recommend the following histories, introductory surveys, anthologies, and bibliographies for further details on the general background and scope of Japanese poetry. The books listed here are in order of general usefulness.

HISTORICAL STUDIES

Varley, *Japanese Culture* (no. **1**).

Sansom, *Japan: A Short Cultural History*. Also, *A History of Japan* (3 vols.), and *The Western World and Japan* (nos. **2–6**).

Tsunoda, de Bary, and Keene, comps., *Sources of Japanese Tradition* (nos. **7, 8**).

Langer, *An Encyclopedia of World History* (no. **9**).

Putzar, *Japanese Literature* (no. **10**).

Aston, *A History of Japanese Literature* (no. **11**).

SURVEYS, APPRECIATIONS, ANTHOLOGIES

Keene, *Japanese Literature*, pp. 1–46 (no. **12**).

Brower, "Japanese" in *Versification*, ed. Wimsatt, pp. 38–51 (no. **16**).

Keene, *Anthology of Japanese Literature*, pp. 19–30 (no. **13**).

Miner, *Introduction to Japanese Court Poetry*, pp. 1–35 (no. **59**).

Bownas and Thwaite, *The Penguin Book of Japanese Verse*, pp. xxxvii–lxxvi (no. **14**).

Rexroth, *One Hundred Poems from the Japanese* (no. **15**).

Brower, "Japanese" in *Versification*, ed. Wimsatt, pp. 38–51 (no. **16**).

Hisamatsu, *The Vocabulary of Japanese Aesthetics*, pp. 1–7 (no. **17**).

Ueda, *Literary and Art Theories in Japan* (no. **18**).

Wright, "The Poetry of Japan" (no. **20**).

Miner, *Japanese Poetic Diaries* (no. **21**).

———, *The Japanese Tradition in British and American Literature* (no. **22**).

Keene, *Landscapes and Portraits* (no. **23**).

Miyamori, *Masterpieces of Japanese Poetry, Ancient and Modern* (no. **25**).

K.B.S., ed., *Introduction to Classic Japanese Literature* (no. **26**).

Janeira, *Japanese and Western Literature* (no. **27**).

Kawabata, *Japan the Beautiful and Myself* (no. **28**).

Hearn, *Japanese Lyrics* (no. **29**).

Blyth, *Zen in English Literature and Oriental Classics* (no. **30**).

Sackheim, *The Silent Firefly* (no. **31**).

BIBLIOGRAPHIES

Japan P.E.N. Club, comp., *Japanese Literature in European Languages* (no. **32**).

Silberman, *Japan and Korea* (no. **33**).

Association for Asian Studies, comp., *Bibliography of Asian Studies,* annual (no. **34**).

————, *Cumulative Bibliography of Asian Studies, 1941–1965* (no. **35**).

Fujino, *Modern Japanese Literature in Western Translations* (no. **36**).

Shulman, *Japan and Korea* (no. **37**).

Index Translationum, International Bibliography of Translations (no. **38**).

II. Primitive Song and Poetry (ca. 550–686)

The earliest poetry of Japan, as of most societies, emerges indistinctly from the mists of prehistory. Dating is a major problem for scholars, and questions are asked about the possible reworking of ancient themes to suit the tastes of later compilers. The *Record of Ancient Matters* (712) is the earliest Japanese record, followed closely by the *Chronicles of Japan* (720) and the first great anthology of verse, the *Collection for Ten Thousand Generations* (ca. 759). Scattered throughout these three works is the bulk of what remains of primitive song and poetry, and they are all two or more centuries removed from what are presumed to be the oldest fragments which they preserve. Brower and Miner tell us that "the queried date for the beginning of this primitive period, A.D. 550, is nothing more than the approximate time at which the Japanese chronicles begin to become accurate, and is not a proper *terminus a quo* of these songs" (*Japanese Court Poetry*, p. 40). Moreover, since such songs continued to be composed even later than 686—the year the Empress Jitō (r. 686–97) came to the throne—this is likewise a somewhat arbitrary date at which to end the period. But since a new poetic spirit was developing at about this time with Hitomaro (fl. ca. 680–700) and others, the date will serve as well as another.

Curiously, the songs and poetry of the primitive period often have the power to move contemporary scholars more than the sophisticated verses of later periods, although for contrary reasons. To some they are the strong spontaneous creations of a people still untouched by the corrupting artificialities of civilization. Others vehemently reject such views as pernicious romanticizing, and see these early statements as no more than the clumsy antecedents of a poetic tradition that came into its own when poets began to concern themselves consciously with problems of style. The reader must choose for himself between the enthusiasts and the detractors. Fortunately we now have the greater part of this body of primitive verse available to us in responsible English translations.

Among the minor works which date from later centuries but are thought to contain early fragments, we should mention the ritual prayers of the Shintō liturgy (*Norito*) and the twenty-one "Score-songs for the *Wagon*" (*Kinkafu*).

POETIC FORMS

1. Songs (*kayō*).
2. "Half Poems" (*katauta*). Syllable pattern: 5/7/7.
3. "Short Poem" (*tanka*) = "Japanese Poem" (*waka*). Syllable pattern: 5/7/5/7/7.
4. "Long Poem" (*chōka*). Syllable pattern: 5/7/5/7 . . . 7.
5. "Head-repeated Poem" (*sedōka*). Syllable pattern: 5/7/7/5/7/7.

GENERAL STUDIES AND TRANSLATIONS

Philippi, tr., *Kojiki* (no. **39**).
Aston, tr., *Nihongi* (no. **41**).
Nippon Gakujutsu Shinkōkai, ed., *The Manyōshū* (no. **46**).
Philippi, tr., *Norito* (no. **42**).
———, *This Wine of Peace, This Wine of Laughter* (no. **43**).
Brannen and Elliot, *Festive Wine* (no. **44**).
Brower and Miner, *Japanese Court Poetry*, pp. 39–78 (no. **48**).

III. The Early Literary Period (686–784)

The Early Literary Period began with the appearance of a group of outstanding poets, among them the greatest contributor to the *Manyōshū* and master of the "long verse" (*chōka*), Kakinomoto Hitomaro (fl. ca. 680–700). The period's ninety-eight years, like the century following the Meiji Restoration twelve hundred years later, saw profound changes in Japanese institutions. In 710 the first permanent capital was established at Nara, which gave its name to the political era ending in 784, when the capital was moved temporarily to Nagaoka before the founding of Heian-kyō (Kyoto) a decade later.

As the special inheritors of the English-speaking tradition, we are understandably intrigued by the coincidence in the eighth century of the *Manyōshū* with *Beowulf* and Bede the Venerable. On the other hand, from the broader perspective of world literature we might note that Chinese poetry was experiencing a golden age, the age of Hsüan Tsung (Ming Huang, 712–56) and his unfortunate concubine, Yang Kuei-fei; of Li Po (705–62), Tu Fu (712–70), and, somewhat later, of the influential Po Chü-i (772–846).

It is one of the ironic complexities of Japanese literary history that a Chinese example inspired not only the purism of conventional poets but also the seeming iconoclasm of poets like Yoshitada.... Known to the Japanese as Haku Rakuten, Po Chü-i already enjoyed an enormous reputation in Japan even during his lifetime. In speaking of the Western tradition, C.S. Lewis has characterized the development of medieval and Renaissance courtly love as "Ovid misunderstood." It might be said similarly that no small part of the history of Japanese Court poetry can be summarized as "Po Chü-i half-understood." [Robert H. Brower and Earl Miner, *Japanese Court Poetry*, p. 180]

The century and a half between the compilation of the *Manyōshū* and the first great imperial anthology of poetry, the *Collection of Ancient and Modern Times* (*Kokinshū*, ca. 905), was dominated by Chinese models. Not only were artistic ideals appropriated, but the Japanese wrote a considerable amount of poetry in the Chinese language (*kanshi*). The first collection of such verse is the *Fond Recollections of Poetry* (*Kaifūsō*, compiled 751), and the first attempt to analyze Japanese poetry in terms of Chinese literary principles is the *Standard Poetic Forms* (*Kakyō hyōshiki*, 772). Centuries later the *nō* dramatist Zeami wrote

a play called *Haku Rakuten*, in which the Chinese cultural domi-
nance is represented as being overthrown when the god
Sumiyoshi blows Po Chü-i's boat back to China.

Although a variety of poetic forms—all variants on the 5,7
syllable pattern—made their appearance during this period, for
most it was a brief one. The "long poem" (*chōka*) reached a
high point of development and then, somewhat mysteriously,
vanished completely (or adopted new disguises; see pp. 16–17
of guide), as the "short poem" (*tanka*) became the preeminent
verse form for many centuries to come.

BIBLIOGRAPHIC OUTLINE

A. *Manyōshū* (Collection for Ten Thousand Generations, 759)
    1. Representative Poets
            Kakinomoto Hitomaro (fl. ca. 680–700)
            Yamanoue Okura (?660–?733)
            Takahashi Mushimaro (fl. ca. 730)
            Ōtomo Yakamochi (718–85)
            Ōtomo Tabito (665–731)
            Yamabe Akahito (d. ?736)
    2. Translations and Studies
            Nippon Gakujutsu Shinkōkai, *Manyōshū* (no. **46**).
            Brower and Miner, *Japanese Court Poetry* (no. **48**).
            Miner, *Introduction to Japanese Court Poetry* (no. **59**).
            Bownas and Thwaite, *Penguin Book of Japanese Verse*
            (no. **14**).
            Keene, *Anthology of Japanese Literature* (no. **13**).
            Rexroth, *One Hundred Poems from the Japanese* (no. **15**).
            Yasuda, *Land of the Reed Plains* (no. **47**).
            K.B.S., *Introduction to Classic Japanese Literature* (no. **26**).
B. Theoretical Works
    1. *Kakyō hyōshiki* (Standard Poetic Forms, 772)
            Philippi, *This Wine of Peace* (no. **43**).
            Katō, "Mumyōshō," pp. 329–32 (no. **73**).
            Putzar, *Japanese Literature* (no. **10**).
C. Chinese Poetry by Japanese (*kanshi*)
    1. *Kaifūsō* (Fond Recollections of Poetry, 751)
            Tsunoda, de Bary, and Keene, *Sources of Japanese Tradi-
            tion* I, pp. 88–90 (no. **7**).
    2. Miscellanea

Keene, *Anthology of Japanese Literature*, pp. 162–63 (no. **13**).

Watson, "Some Remarks on the Kanshi" (no. **50**).

Yoshikawa, "Chinese Poetry in Japan: Influence and Reaction" (see Watson article, above).

IV. The Early Classical Period (784–1100)

The *Collection of Ancient and Modern Times (Kokinshū*, 905), first of the twenty-one imperial anthologies of *waka (chokusenshū*, the last compiled in 1439), reestablished the primacy of Japanese verse and set the direction and tone of the poetic tradition during the classic Heian Period, and, in a broader sense, for the next thousand years. Flirtation with Chinese poetry reoccurred from time to time in later centuries, but never as a serious challenge to the native modes of expression. The thirty-one syllable *tanka*, "short verse" (in a 5/7/5/7/7 syllable pattern), is also appropriately called *waka*, "Japanese verse," since it was the unchallenged poetic form during the Heian and into the Kamakura period. Later poetic forms—*renga* (linked-verse), *haiku, senryū, kyōka*, all closely related to the *waka*—challenged its dominance but never superseded it.

It is appropriate to begin any consideration of the Early Classical Period with a citation from Ki no Tsurayuki's Japanese Preface to the *Kokinshū*. Tsurayuki, also author of the poetic *Tosa Diary*, sketches in a few deft lines the rationale of the tradition.

Japanese poetry has for its seed the human heart, and grows into countless leaves of words. In this life many things touch men: they seek then to express their feelings by images drawn from what they see or hear. Who among men does not compose poetry on hearing the song of the nightingale among the flowers, or the cries of the frog who lives in the water? Poetry it is which, without effort, moves heaven and earth, and stirs to pity the invisible demons and gods; which makes sweet the ties between men and women; and which can comfort the hearts of fierce warriors. [Donald Keene, *Japanese Literature*, p. 22 ff.; see also *Japanese Court Poetry*, p. 4]

Tsurayuki tells us that the purpose of poetry is to express our feelings through the use of sensuous images and in the first line he identifies two basic terms which permeate Japanese poetic theory: "heart" (*kokoro*) and "words" (*kotoba*). For the *Kokinshū* poet the ideal was propriety, balance—neither an excess of "heart" nor "words." And to illustrate his point, Tsurayuki continues the preface by singling out the Six Poetic Geniuses, Japanese poets of the previous century, who in one way or another failed to maintain the proper balance in their compositions. (See McCullough, tr., *Tales of Ise* for the best treatment of the Six Poetic Geniuses.)

Since the composition of *waka* in court society was understood to be a requirement for ordinary social discourse rather than the activity of a few professional versifiers, it is not surprising that we find poetry everywhere throughout the literature. The early "poem-tales" (*utamonogatari*) may be viewed simply as poetry collections organized and structured by the addition of connective prose; "diary literature" (*nikki bungaku*), however else it may differ from mere biographical chronicle (see Miner, *Japanese Poetic Diaries*), is also noteworthy for its high verse content; and the *Tale of Genji*, which we see today essentially as a novel, includes so many poems that at one time it was employed as a poetry guide. In short, *waka* so permeates the entire literary tradition that an exhaustive guide to Japanese poetry would be almost the same as a history of Japanese literature.

Chinese poetry continued to be composed by Buddhist monks such as Kūkai (774–835), founder of Japanese Shingon, and by Sinophiles like the famous Sugawara Michizane (845–903), deified as the patron of calligraphy and poetry. We should also note in passing two influential anthologies compiled in Japan containing Chinese poems by Chinese: Kintō's *Collection of Poetic Recitations in Chinese and Japanese (Wakan rōeishū)* and the *Hakushi monjū (Selected Works of Po Chü-i)*.

GENERAL STUDIES AND TRANSLATIONS

Brower and Miner, *Japanese Court Poetry*, pp. 157–230 (no. **48**).
Miner, *Introduction to Japanese Court Poetry*, pp. 79–100 (no. **59**).
Waley, *Japanese Poetry* (no. **60**).
Keene, *Anthology of Japanese Literature* (no. **13**).
Hisamatsu, *Vocabulary of Japanese Aesthetics*, pp. 8–31 (no. **17**).
Sansom, *Japan to 1334*, pp. 178–96 (no. **3**).
Morris, *The World of the Shining Prince* (no. **65**).
Bownas and Thwaite, *Penguin Book of Japanese Verse* (no. **14**).
Rexroth, *One Hundred Poems from the Japanese* (no. **15**).
Miyamori, *Masterpieces of Japanese Poetry* (no. **25**).

BIBLIOGRAPHIC OUTLINE

A.   Imperial Anthologies of Poetry (*chokusenshū*). General.
      Brower and Miner, *Japanese Court Poetry*, pp. 481–87 (no. **48**).
      Reischauer and Yamagiwa, *Translations from Early Japanese Literature*, pp. 131–35 (no. **58**).

B. *Kokinshū* (Collection of Ancient and Modern Times, ca. 905), first imperial anthology.
   1. Prefaces
       Ceadel articles (nos. **62–64**).
       Katō, "Mumyōshō," pp. 333–34 (no. **73**).
       Brower and Miner, *Japanese Court Poetry* (no. **48**).
       Keene, *Japanese Literature*, p. 22 ff. (no. **12**).
   2. Representative Poets
       "Six Poetic Geniuses" (*Rokkasen*), see *Ise monogatari* (no. **51**)
       Ki no Tsurayuki (884–946)
       Ariwara Narihira (825–80)
       Ki no Tomonori (fl. ca. 890)
   3. Translations and Studies
       Brower and Miner, *Japanese Court Poetry* (no. **48**).
       Miner, *Introduction to Japanese Court Poetry*, pp. 79–95 (no. **59**).
       Waley, *Uta* (no. **60**); Rexroth (no. **15**); Bownas and Thwaite (no. **14**); Keene, *Anthology* (no. **13**).
C. *Goshūishū* (Later Collection of Gleanings, 1086), fourth imperial anthology
       Morrell, "*Buddhist Poetry in the Goshūishū*" (no. **54**).
D. Poem-Tales (*utamonogatari*)
   1. *Ise monogatari* (Tales of Ise, 10th cent.)
       McCullough, tr., *Tales of Ise* (no. **51**).
   2. *Yamato monogatari* (Tales of Yamato, ca. 951–52)
       Tahara, tr., "*Yamato monogatari*" (no. **52**).
E. "Diary Literature" (*nikki bungaku*)
   1. *Tosa nikki* (The Tosa Diary, 935) of Ki no Tsurayuki
       Miner, *Japanese Poetic Diaries* (no. **21**).
       Keene, *Anthology of Japanese Literature*, pp. 82–91 (no. **13**, partial tr.).
   2. *Izumi shikibu nikki* (The Izumi Shikibu Diary, ca. 970–1030)
       Cranston, tr., *The Izumi Shikibu Diary* (nos. **55, 56**).
       Miner, tr., in *Japanese Poetic Diaries* (no. **21**).
   3. *Sarashina nikki* (The Sarashina Diary, ca. 1059)
       Morris, tr., *As I Crossed a Bridge of Dreams* (no. **57**).
F. *Genji monogatari* (The Tale of Genji, ca. 1002–1020)
       Waley, tr., *The Tale of Genji* (no. **53**).
       Morris, *The World of the Shining Prince* (no. **65**).
G. Theoretical Works
   1. Ki no Tsurayuki, *Kokinshū* preface
       See *Kokinshū*, above.
       Ueda, *Literary and Art Theories in Japan*, Chapter I (no. **18**).
   2. Mibu no Tadamine, *Wakatei jusshu* (Ten Styles of Japanese Poetry)

Katō, "Mumyōshō," p. 334 (no. **73**).

Brower and Miner, *Japanese Court Poetry* (no. **48**).

3. Fujiwara Kintō, *Wakakubon* (Nine Steps of Waka) and *Shinsen zuinō* (The Essence of Poetry Newly Selected)

Katō, "Mumyōshō," p. 335 (no. **73**).

Brower and Miner, *Japanese Court Poetry*, p. 181 ff. (no. **48**).

H. Chinese Poetry by Japanese

Keene, *Anthology of Japanese Literature*, pp. 162–66 (no. **13**).

Hakeda, *Kūkai*. See index, p. 298 (no. **61**).

Watson, "Some Remarks on the Kanshi" (no. **50**).

I. Compendia of Chinese Verse

1. Fujiwara Kintō, *Wakan rōeishū* (Collection of Poetic Recitations in Chinese and Japanese)

Harich-Schneider, *Rōei* (no. **66**).

2. *Hakushi monjū* (Selected Works of Po Chü-i, comp. 824)

V. The Mid-Classical Period (1100–1241)

Meanwhile the countries of the Far West were gradually emerging from the barbarism which attended the fall of Rome. Charlemagne was crowned by the pope in 800, within a decade of the founding of Heian-kyō (Kyoto), and the Carolingian renaissance marked the beginning of the rejuvenation of European arts and letters. In England Alfred the Great (848–99) encouraged learning by translating Bede's *History* and Boethius's *Consolations of Philosophy*. Somewhat later, the greatest Anglo-Saxon prose writer, Aelfric the Grammarian (fl. ca. 955–ca. 1010), produced religious works. Romanesque art flourished from the mid-eleventh to the mid-twelfth century, and was followed by the Gothic style (Chartres was begun after 1194). And Aquinas's dates (1225–74) almost correspond to those of the outstanding Japanese Zen philosopher, Dōgen (1200–1253).

From the ninth to the thirteenth centuries, Kyoto was one of a very few centers of culture in the world. In his introduction to *The World of the Shining Prince,* Ivan Morris eloquently describes the situation.

For us who inhabit a planet which, at least so far as communications are concerned, has become a single unit it requires a real effort of the imagination to picture a state of affairs in which men in most parts of the world linger in a state of cultural obscurity, absorbed almost entirely in the brute struggle for survival and power, while here and there, often on widely separated points of the globe, civilizations shine or flicker like ships' lights on a dark ocean. Yet so it has been during a great part of human history. So it was one thousand years ago. [Page xii]

Toward the end of the Heian period, new artistic attitudes developed to accompany the radical social changes that were about to take place. In contrast to the Early Classical idea of propriety and balance, the new mood could be characterized as "depth" (*yūgen*). Instead of a proper balance between "heart" and "words", it was held that a poem would be good "only when many meanings are compressed into a single word, when the depths of feeling are exhausted yet not expressed" (from Chōmei's *Mumyōshō,* as cited in *Japanese Court Poetry*, p. 269). Ono no Komachi and Narihira, two of the Six Poetic Geniuses whom Tsurayuki had criticized for an excess of *kokoro*, were

36

now vindicated. In addition, the poetry of the period was characterized by natural description symbolic of human experience, and a consciousness of the past, which gave to the poetry a complexity of meaning that often belies its surface simplicity and poses insoluble problems for the translator.

The representative work of the Mid-Classical Period is the *New Collection of Ancient and Modern Times* (*Shinkokinshū*, 1206), considered by some to be the greatest collection after the *Manyōshū*. But whereas the *Manyōshū* stood sublimely alone in its time, the *Shinkokinshū* is complemented by numerous imperial and private collections and theoretical works, among them the *Senzaishū*, compiled by Fujiwara Teika's father, Shunzei; Saigyō's *Mountain Hermitage* (*Sankashū*); Sanetomo's *Kamakura Official's Collection* (*Kinkaishū*); Teika's *Superior Poems of Our Time* (*Kindai shūka*); and records of poetry contests (*utaawase*).

A transition from the anthologies of court poetry (i.e., *waka*) to the linked-verse (*renga*) of the fourteenth and fifteenth centuries can be seen in the principles of association and progression by which the *Shinkokinshū* and later collections were structured (see pp. 17–18 of guide; also, Konishi, et al., "Association and Progression..."; and Brower and Miner, *Japanese Court Poetry*).

Imayō ("modern style poems") are folk and religious songs, now mainly represented by the *Ryōjin hishō* (Secret Selection of Songs) compiled by Emperor Goshirakawa in 1179.

GENERAL STUDIES AND TRANSLATIONS

Brower and Miner, *Japanese Court Poetry*, pp. 231–337 (no. **48**).
Miner, *Introduction to Japanese Court Poetry*, pp. 101–122 (no. **59**).
Keene, *Anthology of Japanese Literature* (no. **13**).
Hisamatsu, *Vocabulary of Japanese Aesthetics*, pp. 32–54 (no. **17**).
Bownas and Thwaite, *Penguin Book of Japanese Verse* (no. **14**).
Rexroth, *One Hundred Poems from the Japanese* (no. **15**).
Miyamori, *Masterpieces of Japanese Poetry* (no. **25**).

BIBLIOGRAPHIC OUTLINE

A. *Shinkokinshū* (New Collection of Ancient and Modern Times, 1206)
1. Representative Poets
Fujiwara Shunzei (Toshinari. 1114–1204)

Priest Saigyō (1118–90)
Emperor Go-Toba (1180–1239)
Fujiwara Teika (Sadaie. 1162–1241)
Priest Jakuren (d. 1201)
Kamo no Chōmei (1153–1216)
Princess Shokushi (d. 1201)
Fujiwara Ariie (1155–1216)
2. Translations and Studies
Brower and Miner, *Japanese Court Poetry* (no. **48**).
Miner, *Introduction to Japanese Court Poetry*, pp. 101–122 (no. **59**).
Rexroth (no. **15**); Bownas and Thwaite (no. **14**); Keene, *Anthology* (no. **13**); Miyamori, *Masterpieces* (no. **25**).
Konishi, et al., "Association and Progression . . . " (no. **75**).
Sato, tr., *Poems of Princess Shikishi* (no. **74**).
B. "Diary Literature" (*nikki bungaku*) (cont. from outline on Early Classical Period)
1. *Izayoi nikki* (Diary of the Waning Moon, ca. 1280)
Reischauer and Yamagiwa, trs., *Translations from Early Japanese Literature*, pp. 3–135 (no. **58**).
C. Private Collections (*shikashū*)
1. Saigyō (1118–70), *Sankashū* (The Mountain Hermitage)
Honda, tr., *The Sanka Shu* (no. **68**).
K.B.S., *Introduction to Classic Japanese Literature*, pp. 112–15 (no. **26**).
2. Minamoto Sanetomo (1192–1219), *Kinkaishū* (The Kamakura Official's Collection)
K.B.S., *Introduction*, pp. 116–21 (no. **26**).
Brower and Miner, *Japanese Court Poetry* (no. **48**).
3. Fujiwara Teika (attrib.), *Hyakunin isshu* (A Hundred Poems by a Hundred Poets)
Sharman, tr., *One Hundred Poets* (no. **70**).
MacCauley, tr., *Hyakunin-Isshu* (no. **71**).
D. *Imayō* (Modern-style poems). Syllable pattern: 7/5 7/5 7/5 7/5 . . .
1. Goshirakawa (1127–92), comp. *Ryōjin hishō*
Keene, *Anthology of Japanese Literature*, pp. 167–69 (no. **13**).
Harich-Schneider, *Rōei*, pp. 44–48 (no. **66**).
Waley, "Some Poems from the Manyo and Ryojin Hissho," in *The Secret History of the Mongols and Other Pieces*, pp. 136–40 (no. **67**).
E. Theoretical Works
1. Fujiwara Shunzei (1114–1204)
a. *Korai fūteishō* (Notes on Poetic Styles through the Ages)
Katō, "Mumyōshō," pp. 337–38 (no. **73**).

2. Kamo no Chōmei (1153–1216)
   a. *Mumyōshō* (Anonymous Notes)
      Katō, "The Mumyōshō of Kamo no Chōmei . . ." (no. **73**).
      Brower and Miner, *Japanese Court Poetry*, p. 268 ff.
      (no. **48**).
3. Fujiwara Teika (1162–1241)
   a. *Kindai shūka* (Superior Poems of Our Time)
      Brower and Miner, *Fujiwara Teika's Superior Poems*
      (no. **69**).
   b. *Eika taigai* (Guide to the Composition of Poetry)
      Tsunoda, de Bary, and Keene, *Sources of Japanese Tradition I*, pp. 179–80 (no. **7**).
   c. *Maigetsushō* (Monthly Notes)
      Brower and Miner, *Japanese Court Poetry*, pp. 246–47,
      258–59 (no. **48**).
4. Emperor Go-Toba (1180–1239)
   a. *Go-Toba no in gokuden*
      Brower, "Ex-Emperor Go-Toba's Secret Teachings"
      (no. **72**).

VI. The Late Classical Period (1241–1350; Ashikaga Transition to 1600)

The final phase of the court poetry tradition was marked by conflicts among Fujiwara Teika's descendants for both his material and poetic legacy. Although the conservative Nijō faction won the right to compile ten of the imperial anthologies after Teika's *New Imperial Collection* (*Shinchokusenshū*, ca. 1234), the remaining two by the innovative Kyōgoku–Reizei faction are considered to be the best among them—the *Collection of Jeweled Leaves* (*Gyokuyōshū*, ca. 1313) and the *Collection of Elegance* (*Fūgashū*, ca. 1345). We have already commented on the transition from the imperial anthologies to linked-verse (p. 37 of guide).

The Kamakura military government, which had usurped the imperial prerogatives in all but name after the defeat of the Taira clan at Dannoura in 1185, reduced the activity of the court in Kyoto to ritual functions. A wave of popular Buddhism swept the country and the old social fabric was rewoven into a new spartan pattern which can still be discerned in modern Japanese institutions. Kamakura fell in 1333, but the Minamoto-Hōjō rule was merely replaced by that of another military clan, the Ashikagas in Kyoto. Political and social stability steadily declined and civil wars ensued until the feudal lords were brought under control late in the sixteenth century. The country was united under Tokugawa rule from 1603 until the Meiji Restoration of 1868.

Japanese literature saw the development of serious linked-verse (*renga*) with such sequences as the *Three Poets at Minase* (*Minase sangin*, 1488); "free" or "comic" linked-verse (*haikai no renga*) which provided a transition to Bashō's *haiku* through the Danrin school in the seventeenth century; the *nō* drama of Kannami, Zeami (1363–1443) and their successors; and a mass of Chinese poetry known as "Five Mountains Literature" (*gozan bungaku*) by Rinzai Zen monks at five prominent Kyoto temples (later expanded to eleven, which included five in Kamakura). English literature during the same time span claims *Sir Gawain and the Green Knight* (fourteenth century), *Piers Plowman* (ca. 1362), Geoffrey Chaucer (ca. 1340–1400), Thomas Malory's *Le Morte d'Arthur* (1470), and Shakespeare (1564–1616). Modern English, as we noted earlier, dates from about 1500.

40

The technique of linking verses has attracted a number of foreign admirers, among them the contemporary poets Octavio Paz, Jacques Roubaud, Eduardo Sanguineti, and Charles Tomlinson, who, in 1971, produced a four-language verse sequence called *Renga* (published with an English-language translation by Braziller in 1971). No finer tribute to the flexibility and artistic possibilities of the form can be imagined, and those curious about the Japanese techniques might begin by reading here.

BIBLIOGRAPHIC OUTLINE

A. Integration in Anthologies and Sequences of Japanese Court Poetry
1. *Shinkokinshū* (see outline on Mid-Classical Period)
  Konishi, et al., "Association and Progression . . . " (no. **75**).
2. *Kōgon'in gyoshū* (Private Collection of the Emperor Kōgon'in)
  Wilson, "Three Tanka-Chains . . . " (no. **76**).
B. After Fujiwara Teika: the Nijō and Kyōgoku-Reizei Factions
1. Family Tree

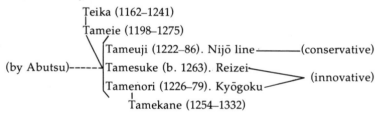

```
      Teika (1162–1241)
      |
      Tameie (1198–1275)
      \  ┌ Tameuji (1222–86). Nijō line ────────(conservative)
       \ |
(by Abutsu)─────┤ Tamesuke (b. 1263). Reizei ─────┐
         |                                          ├─→ (innovative)
         └ Tamenori (1226–79). Kyōgoku ───────────┘
              |
              Tamekane (1254–1332)
```

2. Studies
  Brower and Miner, *Japanese Court Poetry*, p. 343 ff. (no. **48**).
  Reischauer and Yamagiwa, *Translations from Early Japanese Literature*, pp. 24–51 (no. **58**).
  Miner, *Introduction to Japanese Court Poetry*. p. 123 ff. (no. **59**).
3. Major Poets
  a. Tamekane (see family tree above)
    Miner, *Introduction to Japanese Court Poetry*. pp. 125–30 (no. **59**).
  b. Empress Eifuku (1271–1342)
    Miner, *Introduction to J.C.P.*, pp. 130–32 (no. **59**).
C. Four Great Fifteenth-Century Poets (transition to linked-verse)
1. Imagawa Ryōshun (1325–1420)
2. Shōtetsu (1381–1459)
3. Shinkei (1406–75)
    Miner, *Introduction to Japanese Court Poetry*, pp. 137–43 (no. **59**).

4. Sōgi (1421–1502)
   See *Minase Sangin* below.
D. Linked-Verse (*renga*). Syllable pattern:5/7/5 7/7 5/7/5 7/7 . . .
   1. Nijō Yoshimoto (1320–88)
      a. *Tsukubashū* (The Tsukuba Anthology, 1356)
      b. *Renga shinshiki* (The New Rules of Linked-Verse)
         Ueda, *Literary and Art Theories*, pp. 37–54; 239–40
         (no. **18**).
   2. Sōgi (1421–1502), et al.
      a. *Minase sangin hyakuin*
         Yasuda, tr., *Minase sangin hyakuin* (no. **77**).
         Keene, *Anthology of Japanese Literature*, pp. 314–21
         (no. **13**).
         Keene, *Japanese Literature*, pp. 35–38 (no. **12**).
E. Free (or Comic) Linked-Vere (*haikai no renga*)
   1. Major Poets
      a. Yamazaki Sōkan (?1465–1553), *Inu tsukubashū* (Mongrel
         Tsukuba Collection)
      b. Matsunaga Teitoku (1571–1653)———Teimon school
         Keene, *Landscapes and Portraits* (no. **23**).
      c. Nishiyama Sōin (1605–1682)———Danrin school
                            Saikaku (1642–93)   Bashō (1644–94)
   2. References
      Hibbett, "The Japanese Comic Linked-Verse Tradition"
      (no. **83**).
      Yasuda, *The Japanese Haiku* (no. **101**).
      Henderson, *An Introduction to Haiku*, pp. 10–14 (no. **95**).
      Tsunoda, de Bary, and Keene, *Sources of Japanese Tradition*
      I, pp. 443–47 (no. **7**).
      Sargent, G.W., tr., *The Japanese Family Storehouse* by
      Ihara Saikaku. pp. xiii–xx. (Cambridge: Cambridge Uni-
      versity Press, 1958).
F. "Five Mountains Literature" (*gozan bungaku*) and other Buddhist
   Poetry
   1. Major Poets
      a. Dōgen (1200–1253)
      b. Kokan Shiren (1278–1346)
      c. Sesson Yūbai (1290–1346)
      d. Chūgan Engetsu (1300–1376)
      e. Zekkai Chūshin (1336–1405)
      f. Gidō Shūshin (1325–88)
      g. Ikkyū (1394–1481), *Kyōunshū* (Crazy Cloud Anthology)
         Arntzen, *Ikkyū Sōjun* (no. **80**).

2. References

        Ury, *Poems of the Five Mountains* (no. **78**).

        ———, "Translations from the Literature of the Gozan: Two Poets" (Kokan and Sesson) (no. **79**).

        Keene, *Anthology of Japanese Literature*, pp. 312–13 (no. **13**).

        Sansom, *History of Japan 1334–1615*, p. 157 ff. (no. **4**).

        Stryk, *Zen* (no. **81**).

        Stryk, et al., *Zen Poems of China and Japan* (no. **82**).

        Kawabata, *Japan the Beautiful and Myself* (no. **28**).

VII. The Tokugawa Period (1600–1868)

The Tokugawa period brought tremendous changes to Japan. The desire for peace and order, manifest in so many ways toward the end of the sixteenth century, brought a unified rule to the country in 1600. Tokugawa Ieyasu (1542–1616) and his descendants controlled Japan politically until the ascendancy of the emperor in 1868. (Commodore Perry made his appearance in 1853.) At this time the emperor assumed political responsibility in addition to the religious and ceremonial duties to which he had been relagated many centuries before. Ieyasu understood the need for order and in the process of bringing it about, he instituted reforms that resulted in a new mentality in society and in the arts.

First of all, the social structure was clarified and stratified along Confucian lines. Under this scheme the military class occupied the highest social position, followed by the farmers and the artisans. At the bottom of the social scale came the merchants. The Tokugawa social system proved somewhat impractical, for in the long peace that followed, the merchants came to have, in every real way, the money, the leisure, and, eventually, the education. The merchants soon became the major patrons of the arts, and this profound shift from court to common people brought about what Donald Keene has called the "democracy of poetry." *Haiku*, which was developed from a popular form of verse into a vehicle for profound metaphysical speculation by Matsuo Bashō, one of the greatest of the traditional Japanese poets, became the most typical form of poetry in the period. In this poetry was a refreshing combination of homage to the aristocratic traditions and values of the past with a new and wholly genuine poetic vision of the present. Other more traditional forms, the *waka* and *renga*, were composed as well, but on the whole, the genuis of the time was in the plebian *haiku*. Among the dozens of fine *haiku* poets of the period who still sustain their high reputations were Bashō's disciples Kyorai and Kikaku; Taniguchi Buson and Kobayashi Issa composed a number of the most moving poems in the Japanese language.

The second effect of the Tokugawa peace was to slow, although not to stop, the burgeoning Western influence. Portuguese and Spanish missionaries had become an important part of Japanese culture by 1600; in fact, Ieyasu himself knew and respected a number of Europeans. As time went on, however, the Tokugawa family became more and more conscious of the political dangers involved in foreign influences. After a series of insurrections by Japanese Christians against the central government, Christianity was banned in 1637 and foreign contact was outlawed. Only a trickle of information from a few Dutch traders living in Nagasaki in the seventeenth and eighteenth centuries gave the Japanese any sense of European developments.

The natural cosmopolitanism of the Japanese, however, was impossible to suppress. The peace that brought leisure and learning also brought an inevitable interest in foreign literature. Almost nothing from the West was available for study, but the great classics of China provided to an ever-larger number of Japanese a better understanding of Chinese poetry and poetics than was previously available. This neo-classical interest inspired a sophisticated and reflective literature rather different from the work of earlier periods. With the increased study of Chinese and of Confucianism, writing poetry in Chinese had a new flowering. Little Tokugawa verse in Chinese has yet been translated, but what is available helps to provide a fuller sense of the philosophical and metaphysical elements so important in this complex period of Japanese culture.

BIBLIOGRAPHIC OUTLINE

A. *Haiku*. Syllable pattern: 5/7/5
    1. Major Tokugawa Poets
        a. Matsuo Bashō (1644–94)
            1) *Nozarashi kikō* (Records of a Weather-Exposed Skeleton)
                Keene, *Landscapes and Portraits*, pp. 94–108 (no. **23**).
            2) *Sarashina kikō* (Sarashina Travel Record)
                Keene, *Landscapes and Portraits*, pp. 109–130 (no. **23**).
            3) *Oku no hosomichi* (The Narrow Road of Oku)
                Keene, *Anthology of Japanese Literature*, pp. 363–73 (no. **13**).
                Miner, *Japanese Poetic Diaries*, pp. 39–47, 157–97 (no. **21**).

See also translations by Yuasa and Corman (nos. **86**, **87**).

4) *Sarumino* (Monkey's Raincoat)
  Maeda, tr., *Monkey's Raincoat* (no. **85**).
5) General Studies
  Ueda, *Matsuo Bashō* (no. **89**).
  Tsunoda, de Bary and Keene, *Sources of Japanese Tradition* I, pp. 441–58 (no. **7**).
b. Bashō's Disciples: Kyorai (1651–1704), Ransetsu (1653–1708), Kikaku (1661–1707)
  N.G.S., ed., *Haikai and Haiku*, pp. 18–38 (no. **99**).
  Henderson, *An Introduction to Haiku*, pp. 52–71 (no. **95**).
c. Taniguchi (Yosa) Buson (1715–83)
  Henderson, *An Introduction to Haiku*, pp. 90–114 (no. **95**).
  Miyamori, *An Anthology of Haiku*, pp. 64–77, 443–71 (no. **98**).
  K.B.A., ed., *Introduction to Classic Japanese Literature*, pp. 251–60 (no. **26**).
d. Kobayashi Issa (1763–1827)
  Yuasa, tr., *The Year of My life* (no. **90**).
  MacKenzie, *The Autumn Wind* (no. **91**).
2. General Studies and Translations
  Henderson, *An Introduction to Haiku* (no. **95**).
  Blyth, *A History of Haiku* (2 vols.) (no. **93**).
  ———, *Haiku* (4 vols.) (no. **92**).
  Yasuda, *The Japanese Haiku* (no. **101**).
  N.G.S., ed., *Haikai and Haiku* (no. **99**).
B. *Waka*. Syllable pattern: 5/7/5/7/7
  1. Leading Poets
  a. Kamo Mabuchi (1697–1769)
  b. Motoori Norinaga (1730–1801)
    Matsumoto, *Motoori Norinaga* (no. **102**).
    Tsunoda, de Bary, and Keene, *Sources of Japanese Tradition* II, pp. 30–35 (no. **8**).
  c. Kagawa Kageki (1768–1843)
  d. Ōkuma Kotomichi (1798–1868)
    Uyehara and Sinclair, trs., *A Grass Path* (no. **103**).
  e. Tachibana Akemi (1812–68)
    Keene, *Anthology of Japanese Literature*, pp. 434–435 (no. **13**).
C. Chinese Poetry by Japanese
  1. Ryōkan (1757–1831)
    Kodama and Yanagishima, *Ryōkan the Great Fool* (no. **104**).

    2. Rai Sanyō (1780–1832)

        Keene, *Anthology of Japanese Literature*, pp. 436–39 (no. **13**).

D. *Senryū* (comic verse). Syllable pattern: 5/7/5

    1. Karai Senryū (1718–90), comp., *Haifū Yanagidaru*

    2. Studies and Translations

        Blyth, *Edo Satirical Verse Anthologies* (no. **106**).

        ————, *Japanese Life and Character in Senryū* (no. **105**).

        Bownas and Thwaite, *Penguin Book of Japanese Verse*, pp. 131–38 (no. **14**).

E. *Kyōka* ("lunatic verse"). Syllable pattern: 5/7/5/7/7

    1. Studies and Translations

        Blyth, *Oriental Humor*, pp. 245–59 (no. **107**).

        Bownas and Thwaite, *Penguin Book of Japanese Verse*, pp. 138–39 (no. **14**).

VIII. The Modern Period (1868–present)

With the coming of the West and the establishment of the Emperor Meiji on the throne in 1868, Japan changed course again. The pattern of alternating contact with China and isolation was suddenly replaced by an intense contact with nineteenth-century Western civilization, itself in rapid change. The shock was felt immediately and is still felt today.

"Knowledge shall be sought throughout the world so as to strengthen the foundations of Imperial rule," wrote the Emperor in his Charter Oath of 1868, and within a decade, an extraórdinary amount of practical information had found its way back to Japan. An interest in Western literature resulted in translations of Byron, Goethe, and Shakespeare in the 1890s; by 1910, the great novelist Mori Ōgai (1862–1922), who spent his student days in Germany, was putting Hofmannsthal and Rilke into Japanese, while Nagai Kafū (1879–1959), another fine novelist who lived briefly in France, was rendering the work of Baudelaire and Verlaine in superb translation. Young Japanese poets soon had the whole world's traditions and innovations to draw upon for their models. And they proceeded to do so.

Many of the experiments at mixing techniques and cultures proved too difficult, especially as the verse forms of *waka* and *haiku* came to be considered too brief and ill-suited to capture the realm of ideas. The *shintaishi* ("new style verse," or "free verse") that eventually developed as the standard vehicle for modern Japanese poetry is closer to contemporary Western verse than to the forms of Japanese tradition; yet through the use of image and verbal suggestion, some of the old genius of the poetic language remains visible as well.

Among the hundreds of poets who succeeded in modern forms are two giant figures: Hagiwara Sakutarō (1886–1942), whose work was strongly influenced by the French Symbolists, and Nishiwaki Junzaburō (b. 1894), who had a fine European career as a poet writing in French and English, before returning to Japan in 1925 to begin a second career as a poet in Japanese. His translations of T.S. Eliot and his continued interest in the French Surrealists did a great deal to keep the Japanese aware of the diversity in contemporary trends in European poetry. Translators have shied away from Nishiwaki and Hagiwara because their poetry is too musical and at the same time too intellectually complex to render easily—even sometimes perhaps coherently—into English.

The younger generation of poets writing since 1945 have been somewhat better translated, although their works are usually scattered in anthologies that, like some perpetual plate of cocktail appetizers, can never satisfy the reader who really wants to know and appreciate a particular poet. The names of some of these contemporary writers are given in the bibliographic outline below; an hour or two with any one of the anthologies available will indicate dozens more whose work is as personal and as compelling.

BIBLIOGRAPHIC OUTLINE

A. Traditional Forms
1. *Waka*: Two Leading Poets
    a. Yosano Akiko (1878–1941)
        Goldstein and Shinoda, trs., *Tangled Hair* (no. **109**).
    b. Ishikawa Takuboku (1885–1912)
        Sesar, tr., *Poems to Eat* (no. **108**).
        Keene, *Landscapes and Portraits*, pp. 157–70 (no. **23**).
        ———, *Modern Japanese Literature*, pp. 211–31 ("Rōmaji Diary") (no. **124**).
2. *Haiku*: Two Leading Poets
    a. Masaoka Shiki (1867–1902)
        Miner, *Japanese Poetic Diaries*, pp. 199–203 ("The Verse Record of MyPeonies") (no. **21**).
        Brower, "Masaoka Shiki and Tanka Reform" in *Tradition and Modernization*, ed. Shively. pp. 379–418 (no. **110**).
        Henderson, *An Introduction to Haiku*, pp. 158–70 (no. **95**).
        Keene, *Landscapes and Portraits*, pp. 157–70 (no. **23**).
        Isaacson, *Peonies Kana* (no. **111**).
        Ueda, *Modern Japanese Haiku* (no. **112**).
    b. Natsume Sōseki (1867–1916)
        Miyamori, *Anthology of Haiku*, pp. 674–90 (no. **98**).
3. Chinese Poetry by Japanese
        Watson, "Sixteen Chinese Poems by Natsume Sōseki" in *Essays on Sōseki's Works*, pp. 119–24 (no. **113**).
        Keene, *Modern Japanese Literature*, pp. 52–54 (no. **124**).

B. Free Verse
    There are far too many poets for any general listing: those follow-
    ing have by general agreement sustained high reputations.
    1. Early Experiments
        a. Shimazaki Tōson (1872–1943)
                Morita, "Shimazaki Tōson's Four Collections of Poems"
                (no. **118**).
                Keene, *Modern Japanese Literature*, pp. 201–2 (no. **124**).
        b. Kitahara Hakushū (1885–1943)
                Keene, *Modern Japanese Literature*, pp. 205–6 (no. **124**).
                Ninomiya and Enright, *Poetry of Living Japan*, pp. 29–32
                (no. **129**).
        c. Miyazawa Kenji (1896–1933)
                Sato, tr., *Spring & Asura* (no. **117**).
                Snyder, *The Back Country*, pp. 114–28 (no. **116**).
                Keene, *Modern Japanese Literature*, p. 337 (no. **124**).
                Ninomiya and Enright, *The Poetry of Living Japan*,
                pp. 57–60 (no. **129**).
    2. Two Great Poets
        a. Hagiwara Sakutarō (1886–1942)
                Sato, *Ten Japanese Poets*, pp. 68–79 (no. **130**).
                Wilson, *Face at the Bottom of the World* (no. **114**).
                Keene, *Modern Japanese Literature*, pp. 375–77 (no. **124**).
        b. Nishiwaki Junzaburō (b. 1894)
                Sato, *Ten Japanese Poets*, pp. 56–67 (no. **130**).
                ———, *Anthology of Modern Japanese Poets*, pp. 67–83
                (no. **131**).
                Kōno and Fukuda, *Anthology of Modern Japanese Poet-
                ry*, pp. 102–5 (no. **126**).
                Ninomiya and Enright, *The Poetry of Living Japan*, pp.
                79–89 (no. **129**).
    3. Four Postwar Writers
        a. Anzai Hitoshi (b. 1919)
                Mishima and Bownas, *New Writing in Japan*, pp. 205–7
                (no. **121**).
                Wilson, *Three Contemporary Japanese Poets*, pp. 9–35
                (no. **135**).
                Kijima, *The Poetry of Postwar Japan* (no. **125**).
        b. Shiraishi Kazuko (b. 1931)
                Sato, *Ten Japanese Poets*, pp. 30–38 (no. **130**).
                Mishima and Bownas, *New Writing in Japan*, pp. 220–29
                (no. **121**).
                Wilson, *Three Contemporary Japanese Poets*, pp. 39–50
                (no. **135**).

          Kijima, *The Poetry of Postwar Japan* (no. **125**).

  c. Tanikawa Shuntarō (b. 1931)

          Guest, *Post-War Japanese Poetry,* pp. 137–40 (no. **123**).

          Mishima and Bownas, *New Writing in Japan*, pp. 213–19 (no. **121**).

          Fitzsimmons, *Japanese Poetry Now*, pp. 12–21 (no. **122**).

          Kijima, *Thĕ Poetry of Postwar Japan* (no. **125**).

  d. Tamura Ryūichi (b. 1923)

          Sato, *Anthology of Modern Japanese Poets*, pp. 20–28 (no. **131**).

          Guest, *Post-War Japanese Poetry,* pp. 90–93 (no. **123**).

          Mishima and Bownas, *New Writing in Japan*, pp. 208–9 (no. **121**).

          Fitzsimmons, *Japanese Poetry Now*, pp. 120–25 (no. **122**).

          Kijima, *The Poetry of Postwar Japan* (no. **125**).

C. General Studies

      Keene, *Landscapes and Portraits*, pp. 131–56 (no. **23**).

      Kōno and Fukuda, *An Anthology of Modern Japanese Poetry,* pp. xvii–xl (no. **126**).

      Sansom, *The Western World and Japan*, pp. 405–8 (no. **6**).

The bibliography that follows gives annotated references to specific books, and, on a few occasions, to articles that provide information on particular topics. We have made no effort to include every volume available but have listed only books and articles about which we are enthusiastic ourselves (and we herewith apologize to scholars and translators whose efforts we have inadvertently overlooked). Certain important items are not always easy to come by, but can often be obtained through bookstores specializing in orientalia. (Generally speaking, Mr. Morrell prepared the annotations for the poetry up to 1600; Mr. Rimer prepared the annotations for the Tokugawa and modern periods.) Japanese poetry has attracted a considerable number of writers and translators, especially since the war, and enough information now exists that a history of the poetry of Japan can now be pieced together; pieced, indeed, it has to be, since no one has taken on the entire subject in a single volume. Our outline above may permit the reader to construct his own.

PART THREE: BIBLIOGRAPHY

BIBLIOGRAPHY

I. General Background and Introductory Surveys

Historical Studies

1. Varley, H. Paul. *Japanese Culture: A Short History*. Paper-bound. New York and Washington: Praeger Publishers, 1973. xi, 227 pp.

A welcome successor to Sansom's classic but obsolescent (rev. ed., 1943) *Japan: A Short Cultural History* (no. **2**), Varley's *Japanese Culture* is an attractive survey of Japanese history from a cultural, rather than a socio-political, perspective, and is thus of particular value to the student of the humanities. Those who might wish to supplement it with a history of the traditional kind should consult the Sansom three-volume *History* (nos. **3–5**), or the recent paperback by John W. Hall, *Japan: From Prehistory to Modern Times* (New York: Dell Publishing Co., 1970).

The writing is graceful and the format well conceived. The book includes thirty-two pages of monochrome illustrations from prehistoric Jōmon pottery to late Tokugawa woodblock prints, notes, a glossary (3 pages), selected bibliography, and an index. Up-to-date and highly recommended.

2. Sansom, George. *Japan: A Short Cultural History*. Rev. ed. New York: Appleton-Century-Crofts, 1943. xviii, 554 pp.
3. ———. *A History of Japan to 1334*. Stanford: Stanford University Press, 1958. xi, 500 pp.
4. ———. *A History of Japan, 1334–1615*. Stanford: Stanford University Press, 1961. xxi, 442 pp.
5. ———. *A History of Japan, 1615–1867*. Stanford: Stanford University Press. 1963. xiv, 258 pp.
6. ———. *The Western World and Japan: A Study in the Interaction of European and Asiatic Cultures*. New York: Alfred A. Knopf, 1950. xvi, 504, xi (index) pp. (Paperback, Vintage Books, New York.)

The histories of Sir George Sansom (1883–1965) are a part of the basic library of every student of Japan. His *Short Cultural History* first appeared in 1931, and, in a revised edition, is still widely read. The three-volume history of Japan, finished just before his death, complements, although it does not entirely replace, the pioneer but considerably dated three-volume study by James Murdoch published between 1903 and 1926. Sansom belonged to the vanishing breed of historians who believe that histories are written to be read, and his breadth of interest included cultural as well as socio-political phenomena.

Cultural History briefly examines Japanese poetry in various historical contexts, but in the three-volume set Sansom can give more scope to the investigation. In *Japan to 1334*, he considers aspects of poetry in the Nara period (pp. 92–98) and masterfully depicts Heian sensibility (pp. 178–96).

A History of Japan, 1334–1615 describes "The Life at the Court" while the military government ruled the country from Kamakura (pp. 127–40). The influence of Zen Buddhism during the Ashikaga period and the historical background of the Five Mountains Literature (*gozan bungaku*) is discussed (pp. 157–66); poems by Zekkai and others may be found in Keene's *Anthology of Japanese Literature* (no. 13).

The third volume in the series, *A History of Japan, 1615–1867*, confined almost exclusively to social and political affairs, is noted here only for the sake of completeness.

The Western World and Japan (pp. 404–408) is noteworthy for its mention of the new verse forms of the Meiji era, as represented by the *Shintaishishō* (1882). An early rendering of the opening to Hamlet's soliloquy is cited:

Shinuru ga mashi ka	Is it better to die?
Ikiru ga mashi ka	Is it better to live?
Shian wo suru wa	The thing to consider
Koko zo kashi.	Is here indeed.

[p. 405]

In summary, Sansom's histories can often be profitably consulted both on general social context questions and on several specific poetic topics.

7–8. Tsunoda Ryusaku; de Bary, Wm. Theodore; and Keene,

Donald, comps. *Sources of Japanese Tradition*. 2 vols. Introduction to Oriental Civilizations, ed. by Wm. Theodore de Barry. New York: Columbia University Press, 1958. (Paperback, xxiii, 506 and xv, 406 pp.)

A standard reference book since its publication, *Sources of Japanese Tradition* contains several sections on Japanese aesthetics and poetry. The first (I, pp. 88–90) is the preface to the *Kaifūsō* (Fond Recollections of Poetry, A.D. 751), a compilation of poems written by Japanese in the Chinese language.

"The Vocabulary of Japanese Aesthetics I" (I, pp. 172–80) is an examination of Heian artistic ideals and terminology, with excerpts from Murasaki Shikibu's defense of the novel in the *Tale of Genji* (cf. no. **65**, Morris, *The World of the Shining Prince*, Appendix 5, pp. 308–310), and the introduction to *Eika taigai* (Guide to the Composition of Poetry) by Fujiwara Teika (1162–1241).

"Zen and the Arts" (I, pp. 255–60) is a general essay without specific reference to poetry. "The Vocabulary of Japanese Aesthetics II" (I, pp. 277–97) carries the earlier discussion into the Kamakura and Ashikaga periods, with several excerpts from the critical writings of the *nō* dramatist, Zeami (1363–1443). "The Vocabulary of Japanese Aesthetics III" (I, pp. 434–40) treats the Tokugawa period, citing Hozumi Ikan's *Naniwa miyage* on the playwright Chikamatsu's view of realism in art. "The Haiku and the Democracy of Poetry in Japan" (I, pp. 441–58) includes translations from Bashō (1644–94) and his disciple Kyorai, after an historical survey of the origins of linked-verse (*renga*) and *haiku*. Kyorai's "Conversations with Bashō" (*Kyoraishō*) is an instructive dialogue on the techniques of *haiku* composition. (The version in no. **13**, *Anthology of Japanese Literature*, pp. 377–83, is somewhat abbreviated.)

The second volume of *Sources* has only one item touching on poetry (II, pp. 30–35), a selection from the *Sekijō shishuku-gen* (Observations from Long Years of Apprenticeship to Poetry) by Motoori Norinaga (1730–1801) (cf. no. **102**).

9. Langer, William L. *An Encyclopedia of World History*. Cambridge: Riverside Press, 1952. Rev. ed. xl, 1243 pp. and index.

Langer's *Encyclopedia* is a concise but comprehensive compendium of events from every phase of world history, chronologically arranged by area. Edwin O. Reischauer compiled the Japanese chronology, and Charles S. Gardner the Chinese. The *Encyclopedia* provides a useful synoptic view of historical periods and permits their comparison with others, for example, Japan and the countries of the West. Most entries include brief descriptions so that the work is not a bald listing of dates.

10. Putzar, Edward. *Japanese Literature: A Historical Outline*. Paperbound. Tucson: University of Arizona Press, 1973. xiv, 264 pp.

This concise descriptive survey of Japanese literature from the sixth century to 1945 is an adaptation of *Nihon bungaku* (Japanese Literature) (Tokyo, 1960), edited by Hisamatsu Sen'ichi. It proceeds chronologically, discussing genres serially within each period until 1600, and then in a more integrated fashion. A detailed index (pp. 235–64) contributes to make this a most useful reference tool. A short selected reading list of translations and studies in English is also provided. No characters are given.

There are, of course, several sections on poetry, each packed with a wealth of detail not easily available elsewhere, and a sprinkling of examples. Like Okazaki Yoshie's *Japanese Literature in the Meiji Era* (no. **137**), which originally appeared in Japanese and which it resembles in many ways, Putzar's *Japanese Literature* is a valuable source of information for the reader sufficiently acquainted with the subject matter.

11. Aston, W.G. *A History of Japanese Literature*. (1899). Paperbound. Rutland, Vermont, and Tokyo: Charles E. Tuttle, Co., 1972. xviii, 408 pp.

W.G. Aston (1841–1911) was one of the great pioneers of Japanese studies in the West, and his landmark translation of the *Nihongi* (no. **41**) is still a standard reference. *A History of Japanese Literature* is only partly concerned with poetry, and, since both Japanese and Western scholarship during the last three quarters of a century have made the book quite out-of-date, there would be no need to mention it but for the fact that it remains the only work of its kind and is readily available in a recent reprinting.

A Victorian flavor permeates both its artistic and moral judgments and the numerous examples in translation. Aston remarks, for example, that "No Edward FitzGerald has yet come to give us an English metrical version of the best Tanka of the *Manyoshiu* and *Kokinshiu*. A prose rendering must serve in the meantime."

In short, while the *History* is an engaging historical monument, it should be approached not only with reverence but with caution.

Surveys, Appreciations, Anthologies

12. Keene, Donald. *Japanese Literature: An Introduction for Western Readers.* Paperbound. New York: Grove Press, 1955. 144 pp.

Since its publication almost twenty years ago, this perceptive and often profound book (now in its eleventh printing) has attained the status of a classic in the field. Looking at the chapter on poetry, it is easy to see why. Mr. Keene discusses the various styles of Japanese poetry—*waka, haiku,* and *renga*—illustrating the peculiar genius of each of the forms and, more importantly, indicating how a Western reader can set aside any psychological barriers he may have in approaching them. In defining the inner logic of Japanese poetry, the author makes frequent and judicious references to Western art and literature. His few pages on Bashō accomplish what might take a lesser writer many chapters. A perfect introduction to the subject.

This volume does not deal with modern Japanese poetry, but Keene has contributed an essay on that subject in his *Landscapes and Portraits* (no. 23).

13. Keene, Donald, ed. *Anthology of Japanese Literature: From the Earliest Era to the Mid-nineteenth Century.* New York: Grove Press, 1955. 444 pp. (Paperback, Evergreen).

Since its publication almost two decades ago, this has been

the standard collection of translations from Japanese literature, together with the complementary *Modern Japanese Literature: An Anthology* (no. **124**). The selections, from the hands of many translators, are presented chronologically to the end of the Tokugawa period, and a substantial portion of the book is devoted to poetry. A twelve-page introduction compresses a thousand years of Japanese literature into an engaging thumbnail sketch, and the book concludes with a two-page bibliography. In addition to extracts from works specifically classed as poetry (*Manyōshū*, etc.), there are selections from such quasi-poetic literary monuments as the *Ise monogatari* (no. **51**), *Tosa nikki* (in no. **21**), *Genji monogatari* (no. **53**), *Sarashina nikki* (no. **57**), *Masukagami* (The Mirror of Clarity), *nō* plays, *Oku no hosomichi* (in no. **21**), and the puppet theater.

While the *Anthology* is itself a monument of sorts containing an excellent cross-section of the Japanese poetic tradition, it is being superseded by specialized anthologies and studies that are increasingly available, often in paperback. Also, there is the problem of the bald, unannotated translation, discussed elsewhere (see Brower and Miner, *Japanese Court Poetry*, no. **48**, and Bownas and Thwaite, *The Penguin Book of Japanese Verse*, no. **14**). The chapter on "Japanese Poetry" (pp. 22–46) in Keene's *Japanese Literature: An Introduction for Western Readers* (no. **12**) is a useful supplement to the poems in the *Anthology*.

Note should be made, however, of certain items not readily available elsewhere. Several sections of translations by Burton Watson are given over to poetry written by Japanese in the Chinese language: there is the *Kaifūsō* (pp. 59–60), and poems by the Heian nobility (pp. 162–66), by monks in the Kamakura–Ashikaga periods (pp. 312–13), and by scholars and political figures of the Tokugawa period (pp. 436–40).

14. Bownas, Geoffrey, and Thwaite, Anthony, eds. and trs. *The Penguin Book of Japanese Verse*. Paperbound. Harmondsworth and Baltimore: Penguin Books, 1964. lxxxvi, 243 pp.

This is an exceptionally fine anthology of the entire range of

Japanese poetry in a pleasant, inexpensive format. In a concise, informative introduction the editors discuss the nature of the Japanese language, syllable-count, and poetic forms (with emphasis on linguistic peculiarities), prosodic techniques, and poetic subjects and styles—all in chronological order with references to important collections, poets, and movements up to modern times.

The editors have kept the anthology itself as free as possible from distracting (and often intimidating) technicalities. The poems are also presented in chronological order, but without the intrusion of dates, sources, biographical data, explanatory notes, or, of course, the romanized text. For the curious there is a detailed table of contents, and, at the end of the book, several pages of brief notes and an alphabetical index of poets.

We may applaud this attempt to let the poetry speak for itself without the insistent commentary that usually accompanies translations from the Japanese. The English is impeccable (although American readers will be aware of occasional Briticisms: "Three ha'pence worth/ Of fog I saw/ Through the telescope," p. 124). There are times, however, when too little explanation is as dangerous as too much. Bownas and Thwaite's version of Issa's famous *haiku* can hardly be improved.

> The world of dew is
> A world of dew . . . and yet,
> And yet . . .
>
> [p. 122]

But it only begins to move us when we realize that Issa is writing at the death of his child (cf. no. **95**, Henderson, *An Introduction to Haiku*, p. 131).

The reader of Japanese poetry soon finds that he has collected several books on the subject, the better to approach it from different perspectives. *The Penguin Book of Japanese Verse* is sure to be one of the most valuable additions.

15. Rexroth, Kenneth. *One Hundred Poems from the Japanese*. Paperbound. New York: New Directions, 1956. xx, 140 pp.

One Hundred Poems is a delightful collection of translations by the American poet, Kenneth Rexroth (b. 1905), mostly from uch early sources as the *Manyōshū* (nos. **46**, **47**), *Kokinshū*, and *Iyakunin isshu* (nos. **70**, **71**), but also including a few samples *f haiku*. A short readable introduction leads to the poems, vhich are accompanied by romanizations. Translations of the ive-line *tanka* follow no set pattern but may vary from two o six lines in English. Notes (pp. 117–31), generally biograph-cal, are followed by an unusual bibliography containing a large number of entries from the early decades of the century. It s rather odd that the poems are grouped by author, lphabetically, rather than by theme, collection, or chronology; ut one cannot quibble over the arrangement since the translator as done his job well. Several of his renderings appear in Keene's *Anthology of Japanese Literature* (no. **13**).

Rexroth's opening verse, a famous *tanka* by Yamabe Akahito d. ?736) which appears both in the *Manyōshū* and in the *Hyaku-in isshu*, can serve to illustrate contrasting methods of trans-ation. Brower and Miner cite the verse in *Japanese Court Poetry* no. **48**) as an example of the Japanese sense of identity with ature:

Tago no ura yu	Emerging from behind
Uchiidete mireba	The barrier shadow cast by Tago's shore,
Mashiro ni zo	I am startled by
Fuji no takane ni	The lofty cone of Fuji whitely dazzling
Yuki wa furikeru	Underneath its newly fallen snow.

[P. 150]

Rexroth's version is (too?) terse:

> I passed by the beach
> At Tago and saw
> The snow falling, pure white,
> High on the peak of Fuji.
>
> [P. 3]

A third possibility is that of H.H. Honda:

> From Tago Beach I view the sight,
> Above the clouds, of Fuji's brow
> Sublime, all covered with the white
> Of snow that seems there falling now.
> [H.H. Honda, *One Hundred Poems from One Hun-dred Poets* (Tokyo: Hokuseido Press, 1956), p. 4]

No matter which translation is preferred, most readers will find *One Hunded Poems from the Japanese* well worth acquiring.

16. Brower, Robert H. "Japanese." In *Versification: Major Language Types (Sixteen Essays)*, ed. by W.K. Wimsatt. pp. 38–51. New York: New York University Press, 1972.

This is a compact resume of the principles of Japanese prosody by a leading Western authority. The nature of the language is discussed, and a historical sketch traces the basic peculiarities and problems of the *chōka* (long poem), *tanka* (short poem), *renga* (linked-verse), *haiku*, and modern "free meter" (*jiyūritsu*). The essay is highly recommended to anyone interested in the mechanics of Japanese poetry.

The reader might also be interested in an essay by Hans H. Frankel on "Classical Chinese" verse (pp. 22–37).

17. Hisamatsu Sen'ichi. *The Vocabulary of Japanese Aesthetics*. Tr. by Helen McCullough. Tokyo: Centre for East Asian Cultural Studies, 1963. 112 pp.

Largely a translation of portions of Hisamatsu's *Nihon bungakushi* (History of Japanese literature), this work systematically defines a large number of literary terms employed by a variety of authors in different contexts and times. The concept of *yūgen*, (often translated as "mystery and depth"), for example, is traced from its origin in China, through the *Kokinshū* preface, poetry contests (*utaawase*) and through the writings of Shunzei (cf. Katō, "Mumyōshō," no. 73), Go-toba (cf. no. 72), Shōtetsu, Zeami, Zenchiku, and Shinkei. Chapters are organized chronologically: ancient, medieval, recent past, and modern. Appended are three pages of Japanese references, appendices of persons and literary works mentioned in the text, and a glossary of literary terms. Characters are included.

Well written, concise, and useful, this slim volume should be made more readily available. It is a successful attempt to shed light on an area that is murky at best. Without some appreciation of the aesthetic ideals that inspired Tsurayuki,

Teika, or Bashō, we are sure to miss the point of their poetry. Aèsthetics is not just the business of philosophers but an unavoidable concern for every serious reader.

18. Ueda Makoto. *Literary and Art Theories in Japan.* Cleveland: Press of Western Reserve University, 1967. xiii, 274 pp.
19. ————. *Zeami, Bashō, Yeats, Pound: A Study in Japanese and English Poetics.* Paperbound. The Hague: Mouton & Co., 1965. 165 pp.

Japan has produced great art, but little speculation on aesthetics. All art, of course, rests on implicit assumptions that someone sooner or later makes the attempt to formulate. Ueda has brought together a number of these attempts in his *Literary and Art Theories in Japan.*

Chapter 1, "Poetry as Emotional Expression: Tsurayuki on the Art of Lyric Poetry," considers the poetic attitudes of Ki no Tsurayuki (884–946) as revealed in the *Kokinshū* preface (see Ceadel, no. **62**), through his evaluation of the Six Poetic Geniuses (see McCullough, *Tales of Ise*, no. **51**), and in the *Tosa nikki* (see Miner, *Japanese Poetic Diaries*, no. **21**). Chapter 3, "Verse-Writing as a Game: Yoshimoto on the Art of Linked Verse," explores the concept of *yūgen* and the rules of composition as propounded by Nijō Yoshimoto (1320–88). (The outstanding *renga*, composed a century later, is *Minase sangin hyakuin*, no. **77**). Chapter 10, "Bashō on the Art of Haiku: Impersonality in Poetry," is one more helpful addition to the popular field of *haiku* criticism (cf. Yasuda, Henderson, Blyth, Yuasa, and Chamberlain). Chapter 13, "Shintoism and the Theory of Literature: Noringa on the Art of Writing," takes up the *mono no aware* concept as applied by Motoori (1730–1801) (cf. no. **102**) and examines his views on poetry (p. 205 ff.; cf. no. **8**, *Sources of Japanese Tradition* II, pp. 30–35).

In *Zeami, Bashō, Yeats, Pound* Ueda analyzes positions of four writers and attempts to relate them in a concluding chapter, "Toward a Definition of Poetry." This is the kind of comparative study which we can hope to see with increasing frequency as Japanese literature comes to be accepted in the West.

20. Wright, Harold P. "The Poetry of Japan," *Asia* 16 (Autumn 1969): 61–90.

This historical survey of Japanese poetry from the early chronicles to the modernists is enthusiastic and stimulating. Most of the translations are by the author, who retains the syllable pattern of the original wherever possible. An example of this technique is this translation of Saigyō's *waka*:

> Denying my heart
> even I am quite aware
> of beauty's sadness:
> A woodcock flying from a marsh
> on an autumn evening.
>
> [P. 74]

For comparison, here is Brower and Miner's version of the same *waka*:

Kokoro naki	While denying his heart,
Mi ni mo aware wa	Even a priest must feel his body know
Shirarekeri	The depths of a sad beauty:
Shigi tatsu sawa no	From a marsh at autumn twilight,
Aki no yūgure	Snipe that rise to wing away.

[Brower and Miner, *Japanese Court Poetry*, p. 295]

The journal, *Asia*, is published by the Asia Society, New York, to which one may write for copies of the article.

21. Miner, Earl. *Japanese Poetic Diaries*. Berkeley and Los Angeles: University of California Press, 1969. xviii, 211 pp.

In his introduction, Miner contrasts the *natural diary*, the "day-to-day jottings of events as they more-or-less actually occurred," with the *art diary*, "in which fiction or a shaping along lines other than mere fact determines the nature of the creation." The natural diary is a record of fact, the art diary has in addition a "literary element"—more feeling, technique, style. Moreover, "it is certain that the Japanese believe that they have fictional or art diaries, and that we do not. . . . The frequent use of poems, the breaking away from the daily entry as a formal device, and a stylistic heightening—these are the chief symptoms of Japanese diary literature from classical to modern times" (pp. 6, 9).

The works selected for translation are examples of the art

diary, the Japanese poetic diary. Three of the four are well-known literary monuments: *Tosa nikki* (see no. **18**, *Literary and Art Theories*), *Izumi shikibu nikki* (no. **55**), and Basho's *Oku no osomichi* (nos. **86, 87**). The short "Verse Record of My Peonies" *(Botan kuroku)* of Masaoka Shiki (1867–1902; see no. **95**, Henderson, *An Introduction to Haiku*; also Blyth) rounds out the collection nicely.

Poetic diaries are a mixture of prose and verse, and it is the poetic element which justifies their inclusion in this guide. The progressive shortening of verse forms—from *chōka* to *tanka* to *haiku*—was accompanied by "an opposite process of integration of those shorter units," a process to be seen in the poetic diaries, in the poem-tales (*utamonogatari*, e.g. *Ise m.* and *Yamato m.*, nos. **51, 52**), in linked-verse (see no. **77**), and in the organizational methods of certain anthologies and sequences (see no. **75**).

Japanese Poetic Diaries can be recommended with enthusiasm both to the general reader and to the specialist. This is a fine, readable book, and it should be made more readily available in a paperback edition.

22. Miner, Earl. *The Japanese Tradition in British and American Literature*. Princeton: Princeton University Press, 1958. xvii, 312 pages. (Paperback).

This account takes up the theme of cross-cultural influences, this time with a refreshing approach, since Mr. Miner examines the effect of the East on the West. Beginning with early images of Japan in Europe in the late nineteenth century, Miner discusses the reaction of the French to Japanese art, and the effect of the writings of Lafcadio Hearn (no. **29**) and the paintings of Whistler in popularizing Japan.

The book deals with a variety of artistic forms, but the sections on poetry are of particular interest. The long essay on Ezra Pound is especially illuminating. Pound's early curiosity about *haiku* and his famous first attempt at imagist verse in English are well chronicled.

Miner points out how Pound's later work and translations show the poet's continuing use of imagist technique and its relation to Japanese poetry. Pound's fascination with ideograms is also examined. The poetry of such diverse writers as Amy Lowell, Conrad Aiken, William Carlos Williams, and Wallace Stevens also yields a considerable harvest when given similar analysis.

Another great Western poet strongly influenced by Japanese poetry is William Butler Yeats, who, moved by translations of poetic *nō* drama texts by Ernest Fenollosa and Ezra Pound, began the composition of his own plays in the same style. Yeat's own responses to *nō* make up the most fascinating sections of the book.

Added to these highly readable essays is an excellent bibliography of materials available, many of them in obscure places, on this complex and important subject.

23. Keene, Donald. *Landscapes and Portraits: Appreciations of Japanese Culture.* Palo Alto and Tokyo: Kodansha International, 1971. 343 pp.
24. ———. *Modern Japanese Poetry.* Paperbound. Ann Arbor: Center for Japanese Studies, University of Michigan, 1964. 38 pp.

Landscapes and Portraits brings together a variety of essays composed by Mr. Keene during a twenty-year period. All are gracefully written and full of insight; among them, the sections on poetry are particularly fine. Two subjects are dealt with at some length, *haiku* and modern poetry.

The three essays on *haiku* are among the best available in English. The essay on Matsunaga Teitoku (1571–1653) allows us to follow the development of the form from a kind of parlor game to a serious art form ready to be touched by the metaphysics of Bashō. Matsunaga's career perfectly illustrates how court culture was forced to open itself up to commoners in the Tokugawa period. The articles on Bashō include translations of two of his shorter travel diaries, *Nozarashi kikō* and *Sarashina kikō*. Both have been translated elsewhere by Yuasa (no. **86**), but here we are in the hands of a master.

Keene contributes a study on the creation of modern poetry, beginning with the Meiji restoration of 1868 and proceeding through the early postwar years. (This essay is available separately in the format listed above.) Written to provide a general account of the problems and accomplishments of the period, it contains a surprising amount of information, including a discussion of the effect on modern Japanese poetry of translations of French symbolist poetry into colloquial Japanese by Ueda Bin and Nagai Kafū, two important writers prominent early in the century.

A second essay, on Ishikawa Takuboku (no. **108**) and Masaoka Shiki (nos. **110, 111**), discusses the work of these two major modern poets who used traditional forms and focuses on the problems of maintaining and re-creating tradition in the face of artistic and political change. Takuboku receives especially sympathetic treatment, and Keene's perceptive comments on Shiki, when read in tandem with those of Mr. Brower in his longer article on that poet (no. **110**), provide us with a relatively complete picture of the last of the great *haiku* poets.

Attention might also be drawn to an essay on the Buddhist monk Ikkyū (1394–1481) (no. **80**), the eccentric and poet. A number of his poems are translated there.

25. Miyamori Asatarō. *Masterpieces of Japanese Poetry, Ancient and Modern.* 2 vols. (1936). Westport, Connecticut: Greenwood Press, 1970. 803 pp.

This can be seen as a companion book to Miyamori's *Anthology of Haiku* (no. **98**) with which it has many similarities, although the focus of attention here is on the traditional *tanka*. It is a fat, informative collection (although rather dated), with items arranged chronologically. *Tanka* are translated in four-line stanzas, with rhyme whenever possible, and alternate versions are often provided. Considerable biographical data and an index of authors make even more useful this work whose main attraction is the great number of poems and poets included.

The most valuable section of *Masterpieces* is the second volume which begins with Tokugawa poets and extends to modern times. While the early developments in the *tanka* tradition have received much scholarly attention in recent years (see, especially, Brower and Miner, *Japanese Court Poetry*, no. **48**), this is still the most exhaustive treatment of its later phases. There are poems by the National Learning (*Kokugaku*) scholars

(Keichū, Kamo Mabuchi, Motoori Norinaga, etc.), and as many
as sixty-five *tanka* from the pen of Emperor Meiji. Even the
death verse of Ōishi Yoshio (1659–1703), leader of the Forty
seven Rōnin, is included.

The collection, reprinted by Greenwood Press, is now accessi
ble but expensive. It would be a noble deed, and probably
profitable, for some enterprising publisher to put out a paper
back reprint, omitting the large number of monochrome illustra
tions which add little to the book but bulk.

26. Kokusai Bunka Shinkōkai, ed. *Introduction to Classic Japa
   nese Literature.* Tokyo: Kokusai Bunka Shinkōkai, 1948. xxi
   443 pp.

The original synopses of the genres and works treated here
were written by a committee of distinguished Japanese scholars
and then translated into English. The result is a useful, fact-filled
but somewhat awkward volume with an ambiguous reputation

It opens with an eighteen-page outline of Japanese literature
beginning with the earliest records and extending into the Meiji
period. The bulk of the *Introduction* is a collection of discrete
essays on a variety of topics, several of which directly relate
to poetry: the *Manyōshū* (nos. **46, 47**), *Kokinshū, Shinkokinshū
Sankashū* (no. **68**), *Kinkaishū*, the Seven Haikai Anthologies of
Bashō's School, *Oku no hosomichi* (nos. **86, 87**), the Seven Haikai
Anthologies of Buson's School, *Ora ga haru* (no. **90**), *Haifū
yanagidaru* (see Blyth entries, nos. **105–107**), *Wakanashū* (see
Morita, "Shimazaki Toson's Four Collections of Poems," no.
118), and *Midaregami* (see Yosano Akiko, *Tangled Hair*, no. **109**)
There are also articles on works with a significant poetry compo-
nent, some of which are noted in this guide (*Kojiki, Ise mono-
gatari*, etc.).

An appealing feature of the book is a set of fourteen pages
of illustrations: reproductions of famous editions, literary
scrolls, portraits of famous authors, and scenes from theatrical
performances. They include portraits of Ki no Tsurayuki, Bashō,
Buson, Issa, and Saikaku, as well as manuscript facsimiles of
the *Kokinshū* and Bashō's *Sarumino* (no. **85**). There is an index.

Like the Okazaki (no. **137**) and Putzar (no. **10**) surveys, the

Introduction to Classic Japanese Literature will be most helpful to those who are already somewhat acquainted with this topic and looking for a painless way to gather details.

27. Janeira, Armando Martins. *Japanese and Western Literature: A Comparative Study.* Tokyo, and Rutland, Vermont: Charles E. Tuttle Co., 1970. 394 pp.

English literature and Japanese literature are about the same age, *Beowulf* and the *Kojiki* (nos. **39, 40**) both having been composed in the early eighth century. The accomplishments of Japanese literature over the last twelve hundred years have been impressive in every literary form: poetry, fiction, theater, and historiography.

"East vs. West" can be a useful distinction; but it can also have the pernicious effect of exaggerating differences to the point that we feel, often without being conscious of the fact, that the two sides have too little in common to permit profitable comparisons. Perhaps this is one reason that Westerners have made few serious attempts to bring Japanese writing into the common stream of world literature: for most, "world history," "world philosophy," and "world literature" is still essentially "Western history," "Western Philosophy," and "Western literature." It is rather surprising that in spite of a plethora of special studies on Japanese literature, Aston's antique *History of Japanese Literature* (no. **11**) is the only comparable study in English to this new bold attempt by Armando Janeira.

Janeira claims that his book "has no pretensions to erudition or scholarship," but "can be taken as the reaction and appreciation of a Westerner." And most of us will agree that "there is a line where the knowledge accumulated by the specialist has to be taken by the humanist so that wider implications may be found and its deep humanistic value be assessed." Most of us will disagree with some of Janeira's assessments, but we must applaud his effort to introduce Murasaki, Zeami, and Kawabata to Dante, Claudel, and Unamuno.

"Classic Poetry," the chapter that opens the study, is a general essay on the subject, with emphasis on Bashō and a number of his *haiku* translated by the author. It might profitably be read in conjunction with Keene's similar survey in *Japanese Literature: An Introduction for Western Readers* (no. **12**).

Later, Janeira discusses the work of modern poets (pp. 123–34, 145–47, 186–98). To illustrate the effect of contact with Western Christianity he cites short verses by Date Masamune, Rai Sanyō, and provides a translation of Kitahara Hakushū's "Jashū-mon hikyoku" (The Secret Music of Heresy). Other poets are then considered chronologically: Yosano Akiko, Ishikawa Takuboku, Wakayama Bokusui, Sawamura Mitsuhiro, Tamura Ryūichi, Kuroda Kio, Yoshioka Minoru, Sekine Hiroshi, Hasegawa Ryūsei, Yamamoto Tarō, Ijima Kōichi, Tanikawa Shuntarō, and Iwata Hiroshi. Translations are accompanied by romanized texts.

Eventually a variety of such perspectives, as in the Indian parable of the blind men, may enable us to define our literary elephant.

28. Kawabata Yasunari. *Japan the Beautiful and Myself.* Tr. by Edward Seidensticker. Paperbound. Palo Alto and Tokyo: Kodansha International, 1969. 74 pp.

There is no greater testament to the deep meaning of tradition in modern Japanese literature than the statement provided by Kawabata on the occasion of his acceptance of the Nobel Prize for literature in 1968. His speech is virtually a short course in aesthetics, with a great deal of attention paid to poets and their poetry. Among those mentioned are Dōgen (1200–1253), founder of Sōtō Zen in Japan, Ryōkan (no. **104**), and Ikkyū (no. **80**). The short book is well worth reading for insights into all aspects of Japanese literature and culture.

29. Hearn, Lafcadio. *Japanese Lyrics.* New York: Houghton Mifflin Co., 1915. 86 pp.

Lafcadio Hearn (1850–1904), the most famous of the Americans who lived and taught in Japan during the Meiji period, is most remembered for his retelling of Japanese tales and ghost stories, but he also managed to translate a certain amount of poetry despite the fact that he did not know Japanese. After his death the unnamed editor of this small volume went through his writings and assembled all his poetry translations. Long out of print, *Japanese Lyrics* is worth seeking out as a sample of how a gifted Victorian sensibility rendered *waka* and *haiku* into English.

The book has been organized not by poetic form but by subject matter: there are sections on Insects, Lullabies and Children's Verse, Long Songs and Lyrics, Goblin Poetry, and a series of poems translated from the *Manyōshū* entitled "The River of Heaven." Romanized texts are provided along with the English translations, but sources are not identified and folk poems seem mixed indiscriminately with more serious verse.

The English language of the late nineteenth century seems too heavy for *haiku*. Bashō's poetic rendering of the legend of Chuang-tzu (who dreamt he was a butterfly) is, in Hearn's translation, almost portentous:

> Wake up! Wake up!—I will make thee my
> Comrade, thou sleeping butterfly.
>
> [P. 3]

Still, when the image of the original poem coincides with Hearn's sense of fantasy, the results can be striking, even if somewhat stronger than the original.

> Save only the morning moon, none heard the
> Heart's-blood cry of the *hototogisu*.
>
> [P. 9]

Although *Japanese Lyrics* is not an essential volume in the 1970s, it offers a fascinating point of comparison to later and more accomplished works.

30. Blyth, R.H. *Zen in English Literature and Oriental Classics.* Tokyo: Hokuseido Press, 1942. xv, 446 pp.

Even more than most of Blyth's literary undertakings, his early *Zen in English Literature* tends to cause its readers to react strongly—for or against this man. It is in his usual rambling style with countless quotations (including German, Latin, Spanish, French and Chinese) appearing in breathtaking juxtaposition. The academic is suspicious of Blyth's Zen enthu-

siasm, while the Zen purist is offended by his enormous literary
appetite. For others, however, his works, including this volume,
are a delightful antidote to literary and religious pedantry. (J.D.
Salinger remarks in a footnote in *Seymour: An Introduction*: "The
best short Japanese poems—particularly haiku, but senryu,
too—can be read with special satisfaction when R.H. Blyth has
been at them. Blyth is sometimes perilous, naturally, since he's
a highhanded old poem himself, but he's also sublime—and
who goes to poetry for safety anyway?")

Three of the twenty-eight chapters in *Zen in English Literature*
are directly concerned with poetry: Religion is Poetry, Poetry
is Every-day Life, and 'Religious' Poetry. But many poems,
Japanese and others, are cited throughout the book.

31. Sackheim, Eric. *The Silent Firefly: Japanese Songs of Love
and Other Things*. Tokyo: Kodansha, 1963. 203 pp.

The Silent Firefly is an anthology of traditional folksongs,
grouped by region, and enlivened by whimsical illustrations
from Kitao Masami's *Ryakuga-shiki* (The Way of Sketch), pub-
lished in 1795. The editor includes an essay on "Historical Per-
spective" (pp. 183–95) which surveys the genre from early times
(cf. Philippi, *This Wine of Peace*, no. **43**).

The songs in *The Silent Firefly*, such as the one below, remind
one of R.H. Blyth's translations of *senryū* (nos. **105–107**) without
the running commentary:

> Wife and mother
> Are cup in saucer:
> Just a touch and . . .
> Crack!
> [P. 55]

Bibliographies

32. Japan P.E.N. Club, comp. *Japanese Literature in European
Languages*. Paperbound. Tokyo: Kazui Press, 1961. xii, 98
pp. Supplement (1964), 8 pp.

A very useful bibliography, it is unannotated but includes

characters and indices of authors and works. Unfortunately, all bibliographies are out-of-date even before they are published, and the situation deteriorates daily. For items published in the decade since the Supplement, see the annual bibliography volumes of the *Journal of Asian Studies* (no. **34**).

33. Silberman, Bernard S. *Japan and Korea: A Critical Bibliography*. Paperbound. Tucson: University of Arizona Press, 1962. xiv, 120 pp.

In this good, annotated bibliography of selected items, many in French or German, is a section on poetry (pp. 56–59) that includes anthologies, critical works, and translations. Those interested in tracking down early or obscure works and translations will appreciate the sections on Bibliographies (items 9–27: Wenckstern, Nachod, etc.) and Journals (items 28–68).

34. Association for Asian Studies, comp. *Bibliography of Asian Studies*. Annual. University of Michigan.
35. ———. *Cumulative Bibliography of Asian Studies, 1941–1965*. 8 vols. Boston: G.K. Hall, 1969.

The Association for Asian Studies, the leading professional organization in the United States for students of Asia, also publishes the quarterly *Journal of Asian Studies* (until September 1956, the *Far Eastern Quarterly*), the semi-annual *Asian Studies Professional Review*, and the *Asian Studies Newsletter*. Reasonable annual dues entitle members to receive copies of the annual *Bibliography, Journal, Review,* and *Newsletter*. (Write to Secretary or Business Manager, Association for Asian Studies, Inc., Room 1, Lane Hall, University of Michigan, Ann Arbor, Michigan 48104.)

The *Cumulative Bibliography* was published commercially and includes about 85,800 entries by authors (4 vols.) and 83,300 by subjects (4 vols.)

36. Fujino Yukio, comp. *Modern Japanese Literature in Western Translations: A Bibliography*. Tokyo: International House of Japan, 1972. 190 pp.

This recent publication lists by author, alphabetically, "translations into Western languages of Japanese fiction, poetry, drama and other prose writings from 1868 to the present." It is probably the most handy comprehensive survey of translations into Western languages other than English. A sixteen-page index lists the English entries; a twelve-page index refers us to translations from Japanese into French, German, Italian, Spanish, Czech, Hungarian, Polish, Rumanian, Serbo-Croatian, Lithuanian, Dutch, Danish, Finnish, Norwegian, Swedish, Esperanto, and Russian (entries use Cyrillic script).

Those interested in this work can easily obtain a copy by sending an airletter directly to The International House of Japan, 11–16, 5-chome, Roppongi, Minato-ku, Tokyo.

37. Shulman, Frank Joseph, comp. *Japan and Korea: An Annotated Bibliography of Doctoral Dissertations in Western Languages, 1877–1969*. Chicago: American Library Association, 1970. 19, 340 pp.

Dissertations which never found their way into print have become increasingly accessible with the development of relatively inexpensive photocopy processes. Some have material on Japanese poetry.

38. *Index Translationum: International Bibliography of Translations*. Paris: International Institute of Intellectual Cooperation, nos. 10–31, 1932–40; New Series now published by UNESCO, 1949–.

This bibliographic annual of books in translation is comprehensive but unannotated. Works are listed under the name of the country in which the translation was published, and literature is but one of about ten sub-groupings. There is an index of authors. An indication of the range of this bibliography can be seen in the fact that *Index Translationum* 23 (1972), for books published in 1970, is 951 pages long and includes entries from seventy-three countries.

Although one would normally not consult the *Index* before

he had investigated the more specific bibliographies relating to Japan (nos. **32–37, 94**), it has its unique features. For example, Western works published in Japan are listed with author, original title, translator, and Japanese publisher and title.

II. Primitive Song and Poetry (ca. 550–686)

Early Historical Literature

39. *Kojiki.* Tr. by Donald L. Philippi. Princeton: Princeton University Press; Tokyo: University of Tokyo Press, 1968. v, 655 pp.

40. *Ko-ji-ki or Records of Ancient Matters.* Tr. by B.H. Chamberlain. (1883). Kobe: J.L. Thompson; London: Kegan Paul, 1932. lxxxv, 495 pp.

41. *Nihongi: Chronicles of Japan from the Earliest Times to* A.D. *697.* Tr. by W.G. Aston. (1896 in 2 vols.). London: George Allen & Unwin, 1956. 2 vols. in one, xxi, 409, 443 pp. (Paperback, Charles E. Tuttle Co.).

The *Kojiki* (Record of Ancient Matters), completed in A.D. 712, is the oldest extant book in Japanese. This quasi-historical work is usually considered together with the *Nihongi* (720), a history written in the Chinese language and covering roughly the same subject matter. Poems from these two works are known collectively as *kiki kayō* (Songs from the *Records* and *Chronicles*). They comprise the major part of approximately five hundred songs from the Primitive Period (ca. 550–686) of Japanese poetry. (See no. **48**, *Japanese Court Poetry*, "Primitive Song and Poetry," pp. 39–78. The distinction between a "song" and a "poem" in this period is not sharply drawn.)

Philippi's *Kojiki* is delightful reading, in spite of the fact that it is a serious study based on the latest linguistic and historical analyses. In addition to a discussion of the *Kojiki* and its sources, the thirty-five-page introduction has sections on "The Archaic Japanese Language" and "Writing Systems in Early Japan" which are both fascinating and comprehensible to students of Japanese whose specialty may not be linguistics. A somewhat unusual romanization is adopted for greater precision. The translation is provided with elaborate notes. This is followed by additional commentary, romanized transcriptions of the song texts, a glossary of all untranslated words appearing in the text, a bibliography, and a three-page index.

Chamberlain's *Kojiki* was the standard translation for almost a century and is frequently cited in studies such as *Sources of Japanese Tradition* (no. 7).

Aston's translation is still the standard English version of the *Nihongi*, and probably will remain so for some time, in spite of its age. It includes a short introduction, copious notes, and a useful ten-page index. The romanization of poems is usually not given.

Japanese poetry is traditionally said to have its origin in the thirty-one-syllable *waka* composed by the storm god, Susa-no-wo, which appears in both the *Kojiki* and *Nihongi* with minor variations. While scholars have good reason to doubt the antiquity of the verse, its English renditions will serve as well as any to introduce us to our translators.

Brower and Miner:

> I build a covering fence
> Around my home in Izumo,
>   Land of covering clouds,
> A covering fence around my wife,
> And, oh, that covering fence!
>   [*Japanese Court Poetry*, p. 58]

Philippi:

> The many-fenced palace of IDUMO
> Of the many clouds rising—
> To dwell there with my spouse
> Do I build a many-fenced palace:
> Ah, that many-fenced palace!
>   [*Kojiki*, p. 91]

Aston:

> Many clouds arise,
> On all sides a manifold fence,
> To receive within it the spouses,
> They form a manifold fence—
> Ah! that manifold fence!
>   [*Nihongi I*, pp. 53–54]

Chamberlain:

> Eight Clouds arise. The eight-fold fence
> of Izumo makes an eight-fold fence

for the spouses to retire [within]. Oh!
that eight-fold fence.
[*Ko-ji-ki* in *Sources of Japanese Tradi-tion* I, comp. Tsunoda et al., p. 30]

Early Poetic Texts

42. *Norito: A New Translation of the Ancient Japanese Ritual Prayers.* Tr. by Donald L. Philippi. Paperbound. Tokyo: The Institute for Japanese Culture and Classics (Kokugakuin University), 1959. 95 pp.

Poetry, defined broadly, should include *norito*, ritual prayers of Shintō worship couched in antique language and recited for its sonorous effect. The *Engishiki* (Institutes of Engi), completed in 927, includes twenty-seven of these prayers, which are assumed to antedate the compilation by several centuries. In addition to these twenty-seven items, the Philippi translation contains five additional texts: two from the *Nihongi* (no. **41**) and one each from the *Kojiki* (nos. **39, 40**), *Hitachi fudoki* (Hitachi Gazetteer, ca. 715), and the diary *Taiki* by Fujiwara no Yorinaga from the twelfth century. An introduction, notes on individual *norito*, bibliography, and glossary are also included. See *P.E.N. Club Bibliography* (no. **32**, pp. 16–17) for articles on *norito* by Satow and Florenz in the *Transactions of the Asiatic Society of Japan.*

43. Philippi, Donald. *This Wine of Peace, This Wine of Laughter: A Complete Anthology of Japan's Earliest Songs.* New York: Mushinsha/Grossman Publishers, 1968. xx, 236 pp.

"The 313 songs in this volume are the entire body of pre-Heian Japanese verse, known collectively as 'ancient Japanese songs' (*Nihon jōdai kayō*)." They were culled from over twenty source documents, including the *Kojiki* (nos. **39, 40**), *Nihon shoki* (= *Nihongi*, no. **41**), *Kakyō hyōshiki* (772), *Kinkafu* (nos. **44, 45**), the stone tablets at the Yakushiji in Nara (*Bussokusekika*, nos. **49**, ·**43**), various *fudoki* (gazetteers, 713), the *Nippon ryōiki* (ca. 823), and miscellaneous minor writings. Since these verses were composed to be sung rather than to be read, they are classified as "songs" (*kayō*) instead of "poems," although there are few formal differences between the two. Philippi has kept the technical data to a concise introduction and thirty-six pages of notes and miscellanea at the back of the book. Text romanization is omitted.

The songs are grouped thematically into nine chapters, and the translations are beautifully rendered—the only defect being the absence of the original prose matrices in which they appeared. Many full- and double-page monochrome photographs of the Yamato region complement the text. All in all, *This Wine of Peace* should appeal to many readers with varying interests. Scholarly but not pedantic, the results of Philippi's serious research can be read with pleasure. Until recently the early songs have not been enthusiastically received by Western scholars, and we are fortunate that Philippi and the editors of the *Kinkafu* (no. **44, 45**) have skillfully made this material available to the English-reading public. In their directness, many of these ancient songs find an echo in the popular folk-songs of today (see Eric Sackheim, *The Silent Firefly*, no. **31**). When the sea-wife of Ho-wori-no-mikoto ("Prince Fire-fade;" see no. **13**, *Anthology of Japanese Literature*, p. 58) returned to her watery home, her husband welcomed her with this song:

> As long as I have life,
> I shall never forget
> My beloved, with whom I slept
> On an island where wild ducks,
> Birds of offing, came to land.
> [P. 21; cf. Philippi, *Kojiki*, pp. 148
> –58 and Aston, *Nihongi* I, p. 104]

44. *Kinkafu. Festive Wine: Ancient Japanese Poems from the Kinkāfu.* Tr. and ed. by Noah Brannen and William Elliot. New York and Tokyo: Walker/Weatherhill, 1969. 90 pp.

45. Brannen, Noah S. "The Kinkafu Collection of Ancient Japanese Songs" (together with an English translation of the *Kinkafu*), *Monumenta Nipponica* 23, nos. 3–4 (1968): 229–320.

The *Kinkafu* is a collection of twenty-one short "Song-scores for the *Wagon*" from a manuscript dated A.D. 981, although some of the songs may go back as early as the fifth century. (The *wagon* is a six-string horizontal harp, ancestor to the modern thirteen-string *koto*.) In the complete text, instructions for executing the song are included, and the implications are of interest to linguists. But for the general reader the songs are the heart of the matter. The manuscript was discovered as late as 1924 in Prince Konoe's library, which had been moved for safekeeping after the Great Earthquake of 1923 had shattered the Tokyo–Yokohama area.

"Songs" (*kayō*), primitive both in structure and content, are among the earliest forms of Japanese poetry. They are not everyone's cup of tea. Arthur Waley remarked, "Not one is of any value as literature." Brower and Miner are less severe: "We have not become enthusiasts for early Japanese song, and we have not despaired, because we find that it holds an intrinsic historical interest... " (*Japanese Court Poetry*, p. 39). With Brannan, Elliot, and Philippi we come to the bright end of the spectrum of opinion.

Festive Wine is an elegantly designed volume in which free renderings of the twenty-one *Kinkafu* songs are illustrated with an equal number of modern woodblock prints on calligraphic motifs by Haku Maki. It shows a concern for good format which we have come to associate with its publisher, Meredith Weatherby. A brief introduction prepares the reader for the translations, which are followed by a fourteen page "Essay on Primitive Japanese Poetry" and an equally long "Commentaries on the Kinkafu" (including romanizations, literal translations, and commentaries on each poem), and Bibliography.

For most, *Festive Wine*'s introduction to early Japanese song will be entirely adequate. Music historians interested in the performance of these twenty-one songs will find additional information, including twenty-one pages of score, in the *Monumenta Nipponica* article, of which the book is a popularization. For additional information on the *wagon* as well as other aspects of Japanese music, see Eta Harich Schneider, *A History of Japanese Music* (London: Oxford University Press, 1973).

III. The Early Literary Period (686-784)

46. *Manyōshū. The Manyōshū: One Thousand Poems Selected and Translated from the Japanese.* Ed. by Nippon Gakujutsu Shinkōkai. Tokyo: Iwanami Shoten, 1940; New York and London: Columbia University Press, 1965. lxxx, 502 pp., 5 maps. (Paperback reprint without text in romanization, Columbia University Press, lxxxii, 362 pp.).

47. ———. *Land of the Reed Plains: Ancient Japanese Lyrics from the Manyōshū.* Tr. by Kenneth Yasuda. Tokyo, and Rutland, Vermont: Charles E. Tuttle, Co., 1960. 120 pp.

The *Collection for Ten Thousand Generations* (or, ... *of Ten Thousand Leaves*, depending on how the characters are understood), dating from about 759, is the earliest and greatest collection of Japanese verse. It includes some 4,500 poems, mostly *chōka* and *tanka* (or *waka*), with a sprinkling of such other forms as the *sedōka* and short *renga*. The present state of the collection, divided into twenty books, suggests that it may be a compilation of earlier collections no longer extant. The last of several editors may have been Ōtomo Yakamochi (718–85), an outstanding poet in his own right.

The majority of poems were composed within the century and half before the anthology's compilation and bear some of the most notable names in the literature: Kakinomoto Hitomaro (fl. ca. 680–700), Ōtomo Tabito (665–731), Yamanoue Okura (?660–?733), Takahashi Mushimaro (fl. ca. 730), Yamabe Akahito (d. ?736) and Ōtomo Yakamochi. The earliest verse is doubtfully assigned to the mid-fourth century.

Few translations have borne the test of time as well as the Nippon Gakujutsu Shinkōkai's *Manyōshū*, perhaps because the committee had the foresight to consult the English poet, Ralph Hodgson (1871–1962). The thousand poems, a fourth to a fifth of the total, are arranged chronologically and then by individual poet. They are preceded by an informative sixty-seven-page introduction, and followed by romanizations of the text, biographical notes, chronological table, finding list, an index, and five maps. The Columbia University Press reprint adds an introductory note by Donald Keene.

The *Land of the Reed Plains* is a short collection of a hundred *waka* selected from the *Manyōshū* by the artist Inoue Sankō, who published a set of hundred interpretive paintings of these hundred *waka* in 1944. These are reproduced here with translations by Kenneth Yasuda, a scholar also well-known for his translation of *Minase sangin hyakuin* (no. **77**) and his work on *haiku*. Meredith Weatherby was responsible for book design and typography. The book contains a preface, an index of first lines of the English translation, and an index of authors and other items. All in all, it is a delightful book for browsing.

48. Brower, Robert H., and Miner, Earl. *Japanese Court Poetry*. Stanford: Stanford University Press, 1961. xvi, 527 pp.

This is without doubt the definitive study of the main tradition of Japanese court poetry from its inception, through the *Manyōshū* and the twenty-one imperial anthologies, to the rise of linked-verse in the fourteenth century. It is an invaluable, but rather formidable reference work, and the reader may wish to approach it through Miner's *Introduction to Japanese Court Poetry* (no. **59**), which may be seen as an abridgement to make its main conclusions accessible to the general reader.

The text is divided into three parts. Part One (The Nature of Japanese Court Poetry) considers "The Distinctive Common Elements of Japanese Court Poetry," and "Recurring Formative Elements in the Court Tradition." Part Two (The Ideals, Practice, and Development of Japanese Court Poetry) establishes five periods distinguished by various poetic techniques and ideals. (We have incorporated this periodization into our outline.) These are discussed in depth and illustrated with numerous examples. Part Three (The Tradition of Japanese Court Poetry) treats the courtly nature of this early phase of Japanese poetry, its achievements, and its appeal for the Western reader.

The main body of the study is followed by a useful appendix of "Imperial Anthologies and Other Collections of Japanese Court Poetry" (cf. no. **58**, Reischauer and Yamagiwa, *Translations from Early Japanese Literature*, pp. 131–35), an extensive Bibliographical Note, a Glossary of Literary Terms, a Finding List for Japanese Poems Translated in the Text, and an index.

Poetry, more than any other literary form, has an intimate relationship with the language in which it is composed, and its translation poses special problems. When a poem relies on direct sensuous images rather than on linguistic peculiarities or social context, this problem is less serious. In spite of great differences between the English and Japanese languages, it is fortunate that much Japanese poetry does rely heavily on images which can be rendered by an approximate English equivalent. Many poems of the *Manyōshū* (nos. **46, 47**), the early imperial anthologies, and *haiku* have this characteristic, and their translations are manageable.

On the other hand, some of the best Japanese poetry does lean heavily on linguistic nuance and complex social context, and it is here that Brower and Miner can be particularly helpful. The poetry of the Mid-Classical Period (1100–1241), as represented by the *Shinkokinshū* (see nos. **48, 59**), has the objective of expressing the depths of feeling with the fewest possible words. One way to achieve this compression of ideas is the use of allusions to earlier poems and situations with which the audience is expected to be acquainted. Thus, what may appear to be a straightforward and innocuous description of nature may conceal a forest of connotations. For example, a famous *waka* by Fujiwara Teika is included without comment in the Keene *Anthology of Japanese Literature* (p. 194, "When the floating bridge . . .") and in Bownas and Thwaite's *Penguin Book of Japanese Verse* (p. 106, "This spring night . . .").

Haru no yo no	The bridge of dreams
Yume no ukihashi	Floating on the brief spring night
Todae shite	Soon breaks off:
Mine ni wakaruru	Now from the mountaintop a cloud
Yokogumo no sora	Takes leave into the open sky.
	[P. 262]

This translation by Brower and Miner is subjected to more than a page of careful analysis to show "why this beautiful poem has been traditionally regarded as the epitome of the style of ethereal charm" (*yōen*). Many of us have a low tolerance for literary decoding, whether the poetry be that of Teika or Eliot, but it is often hard to see how it is to be avoided.

Japanese Court Poetry is an indispensable book for the serious student of Japanese poetry or comparative East–West literature. It examines the tradition not merely in terms of its own presuppositions and objectives but also in the light of comparable and contrasting Western developments. Even if one does not read the book carefully from cover to cover, there is something to be gained—a proper respect at least for one of the most serious and significant poetic traditions in world literature.

49. *Bussokusekika.* "The Buddha's Footprint Stone Poems," tr. by Douglas E. Mills. *Journal of the American Oriental Society* 80, no. 3 (1960): 229–42.

"The Buddha's Footprint Stone Poems" are a group of twenty-one verses inscribed around 752 on a stone tablet at the Yakushiji Temple in Nara. As literature they are not noteworthy, except for their having been written in an unusual verse form of 5–7–5–7–7–7 syllables in six lines. Students of early Japanese linguistics, however, find them to be of considerable interest. [See Roy Andrew Miller, *The Japanese Language* (Chicago and London: University of Chicago Press, 1967), Plate I.]

Mills has given us a scholarly examination of the poems with elaborately annotated translations. A smoother version may be found in Philippi, *This Wine of Peace* (no. **43**, pp. 91–96).

50. Watson, Burton. "Some Remarks on the Kanshi." *The Journal-Newsletter of the Association of Teachers of Japanese* 5, no. 2 (July 1968): 15–21.

Chinese poetry written by Japanese (*kanshi*) is the subject of this stimulating paper delivered at the 1968 meeting of the Association for Asian Studies (cf. nos. **34–35**) by a leading translator. A selective bibliographical note refers the reader to the best modern Japanese sources, and to the standard but difficult-to-obtain article by Yoshikawa Kōjirō, "Chinese Poetry in Japan: Influence and Reaction" in *Cahiers D'Histoire Mondiale* [Journal of World History, vol. 2, no. 4 (1955): 883–94].

Correspondence concerning membership and subscription to the *Journal-Newsletter* should be sent to: Association of Teachers of Japanese, Department of Far Eastern Languages, University of Michigan, Ann Arbor, Michigan 48104. The *Journal-Newsletter* includes articles on linguistics and literature, as well as Book Reviews, News of the Profession, etc.

IV. The Early Classical Period (784–1100)

Texts

51. *Ise monogatari. Tales of Ise: Lyrical Episodes from Tenth-Century Japan.* Tr., with Introduction and Notes, by Helen Craig McCullough. Stanford: Stanford University Press, 1968. 277 pp.

Tales of Ise is the earliest and most important of the *uta-monogatari* ("poem-tales"). Its 209 verses, connected by prose descriptions of a series of loosely linked episodes, revolve around the amorous exploits of the poet Ariwara Narihira (825–80), to whom many of the poems and the authorship of the work have traditionally been attributed. The *Ise* is connected in time and spirit with the *Kokinshū* (see nos. **48, 59, 18**) both of which are landmarks in the *waka* tradition.

This is a masterful study of the *Tales of Ise* with a wealth of information for the specialist but its scholarly apparatus has been handled in a way so as not to intimidate the general reader. A sixty-two-page introduction outlines the work's social, literary, and political background under the following headings: Japanese Court Poetry in the Ninth and Tenth Centuries (including a useful discussion of poetic techniques—"pivot words," etc.); China and the Japanese Poetic Tradition (The Confucian Ideal, Six Dynasties Poetry, Chinese Influence in the Early Heian Period, The Resurgence of the Waka, The Six Poetic Geniuses, Ariwara Narihira); and Tales of Ise (problems of composition and authorship).

This highly readable translation of the *Ise monogatari* includes romanization for the poems, and notes are grouped together at the back of the book. An Index of First Lines and a General Index are also provided.

An item of special interest in this book is an extended treatment of the "Six Poetic Geniuses," whose poetry was criticized by Ki no Tsurayuki in the *Kokinshū* preface in the process of defining the poetic standards of the Early Classical Period (784–1100). The "Six Poetic Geniuses" are often mentioned in studies of early Japanese poetry, but seldom if ever have they been examined poet by poet as McCullough has done here. Tsurayuki's comments are here laid out and examined with concrete examples. Appendix A is a translation of the "Kokinshū Poems of the Six Poetic Geniuses."

Keene's *Anthology of Japanese Literature* (no. **13**) includes a partial translation of the *Ise monogatari*, and other complete versions are available, but none which more agreeably combine precision and clarity. For another example of *utamonogatari*, see *Yamato monogatari* (no. **52**).

52. *Yamato monogatari*. "Yamato Monogatari," tr. by Mildred Tahara. *Monumenta Nipponica* 27, no. 1 (Spring 1972): 1–37.

The *Yamato monogatari*, "Tales of Yamato" (ca. 951–52), belongs to the genre of *utamonogatari* ("poem-tales"), of which the *Ise monogatari* (no. **51**) is the outstanding representative. This article contains an eight-page introduction to selected translations with extensive notes. Additional material can be found in an earlier article by the same author, "Heichū, as Seen in Yamato monogatari" (*Monumenta Nipponica* 26, nos. 1–2, pp. 17–48).

53. Murasaki Shikibu. *The Tale of Genji.* Tr. by Arthur Waley. (1935 in 2 vols.). 1-vol. reprint. New York: Modern Library, 1960. xvi, 1135 pp. (Paperback editions of the first two of six parts. Garden City: Doubleday Anchor Books).

The *Genji monogatari* (ca. 1002–1020), the unquestioned masterpiece of Japanese literature, is usually thought of as a work of prose. However, it contains almost eight hundred poems (4,000 lines of verse) and was even used in the medieval period as a guide to the composition of poetry. Waley's great translation blends the poetry into the prose rendering, but a new translation—if we are to have one—might well isolate the poems so that they can be appreciated individually.

54. Morrell, Robert E. "The Buddhist Poetry in the *Goshūishū*." *Monumenta Nipponica* 28, no. 1 (Spring 1973): 87–100.

Nineteen *tanka* have been translated from the fourth imperial anthology, the *Later Collection of Gleanings,* completed in 1086. A special category of *shakkyōka* (Poems on the Teaching of Sakyamuni) appeared in the imperial anthologies for the first time in the *Goshūishū,* more than five centuries after Buddhism was officially introduced to Japan in 552. The translations are preceded by an introductory essay.

55. Cranston, Edwin A. *The Izumi Shikibu Diary: A Romance of the Heian Court.* Cambridge: Harvard University Press, 1969. x, 332 pp.
56. ———. "The Poetry of Izumi Shikibu." *Monumenta Nipponica* 25, nos. 1–2 (1970): 1–11.
57. Morris, Ivan. *As I Crossed A Bridge of Dreams: Recollections of a Woman in Eleventh Century Japan.* New York: Dial Press, 1971. 159 pp. (The *Sarashina nikki*)
58. Reischauer, Edwin O., and Yamagiwa, Joseph K. *Translations from Early Japanese Literature.* Cambridge: Harvard University Press, 1951. iv, 467 pp. (Includes translation of the *Izayoi nikki,* "Diary of the Waning Moon.")

Poetry is such a pervasive ingredient of Japanese literature that an exhaustive survey of works in which it appears would be tantamount to a survey of the entire literature. While we have restricted our selection largely to collections of poetry or literary criticism, we feel that attention should at least be called to *Genji monogatari* (no. 53) and certain works classed as "diary literature" (*nikki bungaku*) with high poetic content. (We reluctantly pass by the *nō* and puppet dramas.)

Ki no Tsurayuki's *Tosa nikki* (935; see no. 21, *Japanese Poetic Diaries*) competes with the *Taketori monogatari* (The Tale of the Bamboo Cutter) for the honor of being the earliest extant example of Japanese prose fiction. Miner prefaces his translation with an informative introduction. An abbreviated version by G. W. Sargent may be found in *Anthology of Japanese Literature* (no. 13, pp. 82–91).

Izumi Shikibu (ca. 970–1030) was a noted poetess whose diary is now available in two recent translations. Cranston's is exhaustively annotated; Miner's is directed more to the general reader.

A new translation of the melancholy *Sarashina nikki* by "the daughter of Takasue" has appeared in a well-designed, illustrated volume. It should be noted that Morris's English renditions of *tanka* are given anywhere from two to five lines (cf. Rexroth, *One Hundred Poems from the Japanese, no.* **15**) instead of the more-or-less standard. 5-line format which parallels the *tanka's* 5–7–5–7–7 syllable pattern.

The *Izayoi nikki* (ca. 1280) by the nun Abutsu, wife of Teika's son, Tameie (1198–1275), was composed as the diary of a trip (*kikō*) from Kyoto to Kamakura to settle a legal dispute, but it is replete with poetry. Reischauer's introduction is instructive and the translation detailed.

General Studies

59. Miner, Earl. *An Introduction to Japanese Court Poetry.* Paperbound. Stanford: Stanford University Press, 1968. xv, 173 pp.

This easily obtained, inexpensive paperback is perhaps the best introduction available to early Japanese poetry from its beginnings, around 500, to 1500. It follows the periodization of this historical segment established by the author and Robert H. Brower in their monumental study, *Japanese Court Poetry* (no. **48**). Whereas the earlier work was concerned largely with problems of style and is of particular interest to the specialist, the *Introduction* was written after Miner came to feel that "literary preoccupations need to be tempered with attention to the fundamental human concerns of Japanese court poetry"–a problem which he addresses in chapter one ("Courtly and Human Values") and chapter eight ("Major Themes"). Nevertheless, the focus of the book is still "the poems, rather than social history, literary history, language, or biography."

The discussion is illustrated by approximately one hundred sixty poems or passages accompanied by the text in romanization, and supplemented by a Finding List for Poems, a Glossary, and an Index. While the earliest period of primitive song and poetry (ca. 550–686) is somewhat slighted, we are shown the transition from the courtly *waka* tradition to *renga* (linked-verse) through the methods of progression and association in the later imperial anthologies (cf. no. **75**).

The text is concise and manageable and the book has a pleasant format designed not to intimidate the neophyte. Frequent allusions to parallel concepts, authors, and works in the Western tradition not only make for a readable argument but provide a comparative dimension that permits us to see Japanese poetry not as an exotic isolated phenomenon, but as one more natural part of world literature.

60. Waley, Arthur. *Japanese Poetry: The 'Uta'.* (1919). Paperbound. London: Percy Lund, Humphries & Co., 1965. 110 pp.

In this brief delightful paperback, the greatest Western scholar of Asian literature invites the reader to become acquainted with the thirty-one-syllable *tanka* ("short verse"), or *waka* ("Japanese verse"), through a grammatical analysis of 159 poems—fifty-eight (including four short *chōka*, "long verse") from the *Manyōshū*, thirty-five from the *Kokinshū*, and the rest from later collections belonging to the tradition of "Japanese Court Poetry."

A four-page historical introduction is enlivened by several uncompromising judgments possible only for a man of Waley's eminence. "Of the two hundred thirty-five poems contained in these two chronicles [the *Kojiki* and *Nihongi*], not one is of any value as literature." The *Hyakunin isshu* (see nos. **70, 71**) "is so selected as to display the least pleasing features of Japanese poetry. Artificialities of every kind abound, and the choice does little credit to the taste of Sada-iye [i.e., Teika] to whom the compilation is attributed."

Seven pages of "Notes on Grammar" (pp. 9–15) and a Vocabulary (pp. 103–110) are provided for the reader, who is assured that the classical language is of such simplicity that "a few months should suffice the mastering of it." For those hardy enough to take Waley at his word, a few additional aids can be recommended—Harold Henderson's revised *Handbook of Japanese Grammar* (Cambridge: Houghton Mifflin, 1948) and Ivan Morris's *Dictionary of Selected Forms in Classical Japanese Literature* (New York & London: Columbia University Press, 1966).

The translations, which constitute the bulk of the book, "are

chiefly intended to facilitate the study of the Japanese text."
These are accompanied by the Japanese original in standard
Hepburn-system romanization. The five lines of the original
and the translation are coordinated by numbers, and most verses
are followed by background or grammatical notes. Those who
find this approach rewarding will probably enjoy Harold Hen-
derson's *An Introduction to Haiku* (no. **95**), which includes roman-
izations and a grammatical Appendix.

61. Hakeda, Yoshito S. *Kūkai: Major Works Translated, with an
    Account of his Life and a Study of his Thought.* New York
    and London: Columbia University Press, 1972. xiv, 303 pp.

This is the only substantial study in English of the influential
Buddhist prelate and culture hero who not only founded the
Japanese Shingon sect but is popularly credited with the inven-
tion of the *kana* syllabary for transcribing the Japanese language.
Kūkai, also known as Kōbō Daishi (774–835), indirectly influ-
enced and stimulated the growth of Japanese poetic theory (see
no. **73**, "Mumyōshō," pp. 330–31) through two works on Chi-
nese poetry, the *Bunkyōhifuron* (The Secret Treasure-house of
the Mirror of Poetry) and the *Bumpitsu ganshinshō* (The Eyes
and Heart of the Writing Brush) neither of which is likely to
be available in English for years to come because of their diffi-
culty and specialized appeal.
    However, scattered throughout this study are examples of
Kūkai's Chinese poetry on religious themes. Within the past
few years Western translators have begun to notice Japanese
poetry in Chinese, from Kūkai's to those written by Sōseki
at the turn of the century (no. **113**).

62. Ceadel, E.B. "The Two Prefaces of the Kokinshū." *Asia
    Major*, New Series 7, pt. 1–2 (Dec. 1957): 40–51.

This article compares the famous preface to the *Kokinshū* by
Ki no Tsurayuki (884–946) with another by Ki no Yoshimochi
The former was written in Japanese, the latter in Chinese. Ceadel
concludes that Tsurayuki based his version on Yoshimochi's,
which in turn incorporated numerous excerpts from Chinese
sources. Although "the Japanese preface, therefore stands re-

vealed as possessing little real originality in its subject-matter
and as having a number of defects in its structure, . . . not only
is it probably the earliest extant example of a long passage of
polished, fluent prose in the Japanese language: it is also the
first known attempt to introduce literary criticism into Japanese
instead of leaving it in Chinese."

63. Ceadel, E.B. "The Ōi River Poems and Preface." *Asia Major*,
    New Series 3, pt. 1 (1953): 65–106.
64. ———. "Tadamine's Preface to the Ōi River Poems." *Bulletin of the School of Oriental and African Studies* 18, no. 2
    (1956): 331–43.

The *Ōigawa gyōkō waka no jo* (Preface to the Japanese poems
composed when the Emperor visited the Ōi River) is a minor
work by Ki no Tsurayuki (884–946), author of the *Tosa nikki*
(no. 21) and compiler of the *Kokinshū* (see Ceadel, no. 62, on
his Japanese preface). Tsurayuki's prose "raised the status of
kana writing and was a great contribution in forming a trend
of style in prose literature: its historical significance is profound." (*Kana* is a set of symbols—a syllabary—derived from
Chinese characters and used to transcribe the Japanese language
phonetically.) The text of the preface and of the poems is given,
together with translations and notes.
    The second article discusses a preface to the Ōi River Poems
by the prominent poet and theorist, Mibu no Tadamine (fl.
ca. 910).

65. Morris, Ivan. *The World of the Shining Prince: Court Life
    in Ancient Japan.* London: Oxford University Press, 1964.
    xv, 336 pp.

This eminently readable study of the society that produced
Murasaki's *Tale of Genji* (no. 53) and the courtly "diary literature"
(*nikki bungaku*, nos. 21, 55–58) includes discussions on the social
role of poetry. The several references to poetry (see especially
pp. 177–83) are indexed. For additional background reading
see the Sansom and Varley histories (nos. 1–3).

66. Harich-Schneider, Eta. *Rōei: The Medieval Court Songs of Japan.* Paperbound. Tokyo: Sophia University Press, 1965 *(Monumenta Nipponica Monographs,* no. 21). 132 pp.

Mrs. Harich-Schneider has given us a valuable study of poetry chanting *(rōei)* of Heian and later periods. In addition to a general discussion of the social context in which this art form flourished, we are provided with specific information on poets, collections, and musical techniques. The last half of the study is an analysis of the music, with several pages of score in Western notation derived from the neumes which accompanied the texts in the original manuscripts. The famous *Wakan rōeishū* (Collection of Poetic Recitations in Chinese and Japanese) by Fujiwara Kintō (944–1041), the *imayō* collection *Ryōjin hishō* compiled by Emperor Goshirakawa (1127–92), and numerous lesser-known works are discussed. Selections from the *Ryōjin hishō* are included in Keene's *Anthology of Japanese Literature (no.* **13,** pp. 167–69; see also no. **67).**

For additional information on *rōei* as well as other aspects of Japanese music, see the author's recent *A History of Japanese Music* (London: Oxford University Press, 1973).

V. The Mid-Classical Period (1100–1241)

57. Waley, Arthur. "Some Poems from the Manyo and Ryojin Hissho." In *The Secret History of the Mongols and Other Pieces.* pp. 129–40. London: Allen and Unwin, 1963.

These translations of fourteen pieces from the *Ryōjin hishō* pp. 136–40) are reprinted from Waley's article in the *Journal f the Royal Asiatic Society* for April, 1921. Six of them constitute he *Ryōjin hishō* entry in Keene's *Anthology of Japanese Literature* no. **13**).

We might also call attention to two additional items in this liverse miscellany: "The Ainu Epic" (pp. 194–208) and "Ainu jong" (pp. 209–210). Although the Ainu are racially and linguist-cally distinct from the Japanese, what remains of their poetry s as appropriate to mention here as anywhere.

58. Saigyō. *The Sanka Shu: "The Mountain Hermitage".* Tr. by H.H. Honda. Tokyo: Hokuseido Press, 1971. vi, 281 pp.

Sankashū is a private collection of *tanka* by the famous poet-)riest Saigyō (1118–70), whose life-style Bashō took as his ideal. Honda has given us a straightforward translation of all 1552 numbered verses in his characteristic four-line format but with-)ut rhyming. There is a brief biographical sketch in the introduc-ion; poems are without annotations, romanizations, or index.

59. Brower, Robert H., and Miner, Earl. *Fujiwara Teika's Superior Poems of Our Time: A Thirteenth-Century Poetic Treatise and Sequence.* Stanford: Stanford University Press; Tokyo: University of Tokyo Press, 1967. xi, 148 pp.

In 1209 Fujiwara Teika [Fujiwara no Sadaie], the outstanding scholar and arbiter of poetic taste of the early Kamakura period, wrote the *Kindai shūka* (Superior Poems of Our Time), a short prefatory essay to a sequence of eighty-three exemplary *tanka* for the military dictator, Minamoto Sanetomo. Its translation (with an introduction, notes, bibliography, glossary, and index of first lines) is a brief but important contribution to the research on early Japanese poetry. (See also nos. **48**, **59**, **72**.)

"To teach Sanetomo what was central to Japanese poetry and to inculcate artistic control, Teika turned to the method of teaching by example, a method practiced for centuries in China and Japan by master artists. The theory behind the practice is very simple: one learns by doing, and one learns to do well by imitating the achievements of the great" (p. 15). Thus, although the work is billed as a "poetic treatise" in the translation's subtitle, we do not find here a formal exposition of the principles of Japanese poetics. "Teika's essay is not an anatomy of poetry; it relies upon examples and ideals rather than critical terminology and analysis. In these respects it is typical both of its age and of a major strain of Japanese poetic criticism" (p. 20). (Criticism by example, however, can be the despair of commentators. "What, precisely, is meant by *yūgen?*")

The poetic sequence is ordered by the techniques of progression and association which the authors have discussed at length in other works. The poems are presented with the romanized text on the facing page, and their relationship to other parts of the sequence is indicated by an analysis of "Space," "Time," and "Motifs" following each verse.

Although this is an impressive piece of scholarship and of great interest to the specialist, it reads well and has much to recommend to the general reader.

70. Fujiwara no Sadaie [Fujiwara Teika]. *One Hundred Poets: A Japanese Anthology*. Tr. by Grant Sharman. Los Angeles: Monograph Committee (P.O. Box 2928, Hollywood Station), 1965. 29 pp.

71. ———. *Hyakunin-Isshu and Nori no Hatsune*. Tr. by Clay MacCauley. Yokohama: Kelly and Walsh, 1917.

Fujiwara Teika (or Sadaie, 1162–1241) was the leading authority on poetry in his own day, and probably in the entire history of Japanese literature. It is only natural, then, that the *Hyakunin isshu* is ascribed to him, just as the *I-ro-ha Uta* is credited to the famous cleric, Kōbō Daishi (see no. **61**).

The *Hyakunin isshu* is a sequence of poems by each of a

hundred representative poets, ostensibly selected as models of excellence, in spite of the unfavorable assessment by Waley (see no. **60**, *Japanese Poetry: The Uta*) and others. The short anthology is known primarily through its association with the ritual card-matching game and, in Chamberlain's words, it "has long enjoyed exceptional favour with the public at large,—so much so that every one having a tincture of education knows it by heart; but the native critics justly refuse to endorse this superficial popular verdict" (Basil Hall Chamberlain, *Japanese Things* [Tokyo, and Rutland, Vt.: Charles E. Tuttle Co., 1971], p. 378. This is a reprint of *Things Japanese*, a lively handbook of traditional Japan as seen by the great nineteenth-century scholar; see *Kojiki*, nos. **39, 40**.)

The MacCauley translation is frequently cited but seldom seen. The Grant Sharman version includes a short introduction and notes, with the Japanese text in addition to romanization. The translations are often interesting and somewhat eccentric. Compare, for example, two versions of a poem by Mibu no Tadamine:

It's love, they all say,	They say I'm in love—
And my name even so soon	The rumor is already
Has come up in it.	In circulation;
People would never notice,	Yet when I began to love
I thought when it began, still ...	There was not a soul who knew.
[*One Hundred Poets*, p. 15]	[Keene, *Anthology of Japanese Literature*, p. 94]

72. Brower, Robert H. " 'Ex-Emperor Go-Toba's Secret Teachings' : *Go-Toba no in Gokuden.*" *Harvard Journal of Asiatic Studies* 32 (1972): 5–70.

This is a scholarly and elaborately noted translation of a short poetic treatise by Emperor Go-Toba (1180–1239), a contemporary of Teika and Shunzei in the age of the *Shinkokinshū*. "Perhaps the most talented of Japan's many poet-emperors, Go-Toba was also an astute and sensitive critic. And one of the most important critical documents of the early thirteenth century is his 'Secret Teachings'. . . . For not only is the treatise of considerable intrinsic interest and value as poetic criticism; it is a forceful and telling attack upon Teika's personal idiosyncrasies and critical attitudes ... " [p. 5].

73. Katō, Hilda. "The *Mumyōshō* of Kamo no Chōmei and its Significance in Japanese Literature (together with an English translation of the *Mumyōshō*)." *Monumenta Nipponica* 23, nos. 3–4 (1968): 321–430.

Kamo no Chōmei (1154–1216) is widely known as the author of the *Hōjōki* (An Account of My Hut. See no. 13, *Anthology of Japanese Literature*, pp. 197–212). He also wrote the *Mumyōshō* (Anonymous Notes), one of the most significant poetic treatises in the history of Japanese literature. In the introduction to this complete annotated translation, Katō discusses not only Chōmei and his views, but surveys the history of the development of *karon* (essays on poetry) and aesthetic theory up to his time.

Chōmei was contemporary with Shunzei, Teika, and Saigyō, in the age dominated by the ideal of *yūgen* (mystery and depth). Japanese poets have shown little interest in literary theory, and the *Mumyōshō* is one of the most lucid attempts to define the elusive poetic standards of the Mid-Classical period:

... according to the views of those who have penetrated into the realm of *yūgen*, the importance lies in *yojō*, which is not stated in words and an atmosphere that is not revealed through the form of the poem.... On an autumn evening, for example, there is no color in the sky, nor any sound, and although we cannot give a definite reason for it, we are somehow moved to tears. A person lacking in sensitivity finds nothing particular in such a sight, he just admires the cherry blossoms and scarlet autumn leaves that he can see with his own eyes.... How can such things be easily learned or stated precisely in words? You can only comprehend them for yourself.... Completely to display your feelings in words by saying of the moon that it is bright, or by praising the cherry blossoms, declaring that they are pretty, how can that be difficult? ... Only when many ideas are compressed in one word, when without displaying it you exhaust your mind in all its depth and you imagine the imperceptible, when commonplace things are used to display beauty and in a style of naivete an idea is developed to the limit, only then, when thinking does not lead anywhere and words are inadequate, should you express your feelings by this method which has the capacity to move heaven and earth and the power to touch the gods and spirits. [Pp. 408–9; cf. *Japanese Court Poetry*, no. **48**, pp. 268–69]

The *Mumyōshō* can be recommended without reservation to the general reader as well as to the specialist. Katō's article and translation are important contributions to scholarship, and they read well.

74. Shikishi (Princess). *Poems of Princess Shikishi.* Tr. by Sato Hiroaki. Paperbound. Hanover, N.H. : Granite Publications, 1973. 18 pp., unnumbered.

A slender selection of twelve seasonal poems by Princess Shikishi (d. 1201) which appears in the *Shinkokinshū* has been translated without annotations.

The pronunciation of the poet's name frequently appears as Princess Shokushi, but either is acceptable.

75. Konishi Jin'ichi; Brower, Robert H.; and Miner, Earl. "Association and Progression: Principles of Integration in Anthologies and Sequences of Japanese Court Poetry, A. D. 900–1350." *Harvard Journal of Asiatic Studies* 21 (1958): 67–127.

This article finds in the *Shinkokinshū* (ca. 1206) and later imperial anthologies the associative techniques that transformed them from arbitrary collections of discrete poems to integrated compilations, and provided the transition to linked-verse (see no. **77**, *Minase sangin hyakuin*). The substance of this article has been incorporated into Brower and Miner's *Japanese Court Poetry* (no. **48**).

VI. The Late Classical Period (1241–1350; Ashikaga Transition to 1600)

76. Wilson, William Ritchie. "Three Tanka-Chains from the Private Collection of the Emperor Kōgon'in." *Monumenta Nipponica* 24, nos. 1–2 (1969): pp. 21–29.

Examples are given from the *Kōgon'in gyoshū* to show the integrating techniques employed in the later anthologies and sequences of Japanese court poetry (see Konishi, et al., "Association and Progression . . . " no. **75**). Emperor Kōgon (1313–64, r. 1331–33) had a major hand in the compilation of the *Fūgashū* (Collection of Elegance), one of the two collections compiled by the innovative Kyōgoku–Reizei faction (see p. 40 of guide).

77. *Minase Sangin Hyakuin: A Poem of One Hundred Links Composed by Three Poets at Minase.* Tr. by Kenneth Yasuda. Tokyo: Kogakusha, 1956. xi, 72 pp.

Beginning with the disappearance of the *chōka* ("long poem") after the *Manyōshū* (nos. **46, 47**), Japanese verse tended to get progressively shorter, first with the thirty-one-syllable *tanka* in the Heian period, and then with the seventeen-syllable *haiku* in the Tokugawa. Various techniques, however, were employed to compensate for this lack of an extended verse form: poetry contests (*utaawase*), the use of associative devices in the imperial poetry anthologies (see Konishi, et al, eds., "Association and Progression: Principles of Integration in Anthologies and Sequences of Japanese Court Poetry, A.D. 900–1350", no. **75**), and, influenced by these, the linked-verse (*renga*) of the Ashikaga period. What might appear at first glance as sequences of discrete items were, in fact, integrated wholes—long poems. (Linked-verse can also be seen as the transition between the tradition of court poetry as represented by the imperial anthologies, and *haiku* or *hokku*, the "opening stanza" of a *renga* chain.)

The most famous of the linked-verse sequences is "Three Poets at Minase," composed in 1488 by Sōgi and his companions at a site on the Minase river where there once stood a palace belonging to the Emperor Gotoba (1180–1239), himself a famous poet (see Brower, "Ex-Emperor Go-Toba's Secret Teachings," no. 72). It is an example of a complex art form, circumscribed by numerous rules, which are elucidated by Yasuda in the introduction to his translation. As these rules became relaxed, the "free" or "comic" (*haikai*) variety of *renga* evolved or, perhaps, *de*-volved (see Hibbett, "The Japanese Comic Linked-Verse Tradition," no. 83).

Kenneth Yasuda's excellent study is the most thorough—and virtually the only—treatment of "serious" linked-verse. The entire sequence is translated and each verse is accompanied by a note on the facing page explaining the transition. Appended are the Japanese text with romanization and notes to Japanese sources. The only problem with this work is that it is hard to find.

The *Anthology of Japanese Literature* (no. 13) includes Keene's translation of half of *Minase sangin*; *Japanese Literature: An Introduction for Western Readers* (no. 12), a short discussion (pp. 35–38).

78. Ury, Marian. *Poems of the Five Mountains: An Introduction to the Literature of the Zen Monasteries.* Forthcoming. (Contact Asia Society, New York, for publication information.)

79. ———. "Translations from the Literature of the *Gozan*: Two Poets." *Literature East & West* 15, no. 4 and 16, nos. 1 and 2 (Combine Issue): 694–700.

Poems of the Five Mountains is the first extensive anthology of translations of Japanese poetry written in Chinese and classed as *gozan bungaku*, composed mainly in the Ashikaga period by Rinzai Zen monks at five officially designated Kyoto temples and their subsidiaries. (The number was later increased; see no. 4, *History of Japan 1334–1615*, p. 157 ff.) Sixteen poets are represented by some seventy verses, with biographical and explanatory notes. The volume begins with a brief introduction to the genre and social background, and concludes with a finding list and bibliography. It is illustrated throughout with examples of the poets' calligraphy. Five of the translations appeared earlier in the *Literature East & West* article.

Most of the poems are on secular subjects, in contrast to the selection available to us from Ikkyū's *Kyōunshū* (no. **80**). Kokan Shiren (1278–1346) thus comments on a common Japanese phenomenon.

> That which was fixed, moves; the hard becomes soft.
> The earth is like waves, my house like a boat.
> A time of dread, but also of charm:
> Wind bells chime without rest, though there's no wind.
> ["The Earthquake," p. 22]

80. Arntzen, Sonja. *Ikkyū Sōjun: A Zen Monk and his Poetry*. Paperbound. Bellingham, Wash.: Western Washington State College, 1973. x, 171 pp.

These fifty-five translations of short verses in Chinese by the eccentric Zen monk Ikkyū (1394–1481) are mostly from his *Crazy Cloud Anthology* (*Kyōunshū*). They include poems about Zen, Criticism and Protest, and Love, each accompanied by Chinese text, Japanese romanization, and explanatory notes. The translations are prefaced by chapters on Ikkyū and his times, and followed by reference notes, index of first lines, and bibliography. Seven full-page monochrome reproductions of artifacts of and by Ikkyū contribute to make this a fine introduction to a poet whose name is well known to students of Japan, but not his literary work. This volume may be purchased at a reasonable price from Western Washington State College, Bellingham, Washington 98225.

81. Stryk, Lucien, and Ikemoto Takashi. *Zen: Poems, Prayers, Sermons, Anecdotes, Interviews*. Garden City: Doubleday & Co., 1965. xxxvii, 160 pp. (Paperback).

82. Stryk, Lucian; Ikemoto Takashi; and Takayama Taigan. *Zen Poems of China and Japan*. Paperbound. Garden City: Doubleday, Anchor Press, 1973. li, 143 pp.

An American poet, a Japanese Professor of English, and a Zen Master have collaborated on these interesting books of Zen miscellanea. In the earlier volume is a section on poems by a number of Zen Masters from Dōgen (1200–1253) to the present (pp. 3–33). The bulk of the recent work is 151 brief verses by Chinese and Japanese poets rarely appearing in standard academic collections. A foreword, an introduction, and a preface (on Zen Poetry) by the three authors, and forty-eight pages of explanatory notes accompany the translations.

83. Hibbett, Howard S. "The Japanese Comic Linked-Verse Tradition." *Harvard Journal of Asiatic Studies* 23 (1960–61): 76–92.

The "free" or "comic" (*haikai*) *renga*, characterized by an almost complete absence of rules, was indulged in by the famous poet-novelist Ihara Saikaku (1642–93) in poetic marathons. (Cf. Kenneth Yasuda, *Minase Sangin Hyakuin*, no. 77, for the earlier "serious" *renga*.) The "comic" linked-verse provided a transition to Bashō's *haiku* in the seventeenth century (see p. 40 of guide).

VII.   The Tokugawa Period (1600–1868)

Individual Poets

84.   Chamberlain, Basil Hall. "Bashō and the Poetical Epigram." *Transactions of the Asiatic Society of Japan* 30, no. 2 (1902): 243–62.

B. H. Chamberlain, a well-known professor at the University of Tokyo in the 1880s and one of the first serious Western students of Japanese literature, addressed himself to the subject of *haiku* in general and Bashō in particular in this long article written in 1901. His Victorian mentality is obvious in his use of the word "epigram" to describe *haiku*; indeed, certain aspects of Japanese poetry seemed repellant, or, worse, trivial to him. In his brief account of poetry before the Tokugawa period, for example, he found the formal quality of the *utaawase* (poetry contest) "puerile," and the ribald nature of some early Tokugawa verse made him distinctly uneasy.

Nevertheless, there is much to admire here. Chamberlain's grasp of the beauty of allusiveness is sure, and his explanation of Bashō as a pilgrim in search of enlightenment is deft and moving. He cannot, of course, abandon his own heritage lightly. "Bashō was not born under the same lucky star as Wordsworth. He inherited a language incomparably inferior as a vehicle for poetry and was restricted to a single form of verse, and that the poorest." Chamberlain wished to find the truth of the poet as a man, and in praising Bashō for his "contempt for shams and triviality of every kind," he is well on the way to penetrating the character of the poet.

Chamberlain also includes a discussion of later *haiku* poets, including Kaga no Chiyo (1702–1775), greatest of the Tokugawa women poets. Her work is little dealt with elsewhere in English.

This article is well worth seeking out, both as a trenchant example of the history of shifting tastes between East and West, and for the often accurate information it contains.

85.   Matsuo Bashō. *Monkey's Raincoat*. Tr. by Maeda Cana. New York: Mushinsha/Grossman Publishers, 1973. xxx, 107 pp. (Paperback).

Sarumino (Monkey's Raincoat), published in 1691, is usually
considered the finest of the *haikai* anthologies compiled by Bashō
and his pupils. The full anthology contains four linked-verse
sequences (thirty-six verses in each sequence) and a number
of individual *haiku* by a variety of poets. Although this volume
by Maeda omits the individual *haiku*, it provides an invaluable
sample of *haikai* composed by multiple authors, which is such
a remarkable development in poetry. Along with a translation
of each verse, Mrs. Maeda has identified its author and included
a prose commentary on the poem itself.

Maeda likens linked-verse to a montage, and her spare transla-
tions of these individual scenes are usually successful in those
terms. However, the effect is often overly cryptic unless the
accompanying prose explanation is read with care. Ueda
Makoto's fine short biography of Bashō (no. **89**) also contains
a translation of the second of these sequences, "Summer Moon,"
and a reading of the two versions side by side will show how
different a point of view can be legitimately taken. For example,
Bashō's verse

> kono suji wa
> gin no mishirazu
> fujiyūsa yo

is rendered by Ueda as:

> Those who live in this area
> Have never seen a silver coin.
> What a wretched place!
> [*Matsuo Bashō*, p. 107]

Maeda's version is terse, more accurate, but a bit confusing:

> along this route
> even silver is strange
> how inconvenient
> [P. 48]

Either translation may be preferred for different reasons, but
Maeda's versions are sometimes unnecessarily baffling when
compared with the originals (unfortunately *not* included, even
in romanized form). The same point can be made by comparing
Maeda's translation of the first sequence, "Winter's First
Shower," with a translation in *Haikai and Haiku* (no. **99**). Mrs.
Maeda's theory of *haiku* translation, incidentally, is available,

decked out in the formidable dress—detractors might say disguise—of contemporary linguistics, in an article "On Translating the *Haiku* Form" (*Harvard Journal of Asiatic Studies* 29 (1969): 131–68). The discussion is too technical to recommend to the uninitiated.

The book has charming illustrations and a graceful introduction to Bashō's poetics; while not surpassing the discussion in *Haikai and Haiku* (no. 99), Maeda's comments are nevertheless precise and observant.

86. Matsuo Bashō. *The Narrow Road to the Deep North and Other Travel Sketches*. Tr. by Yuasa Nobuyuki. Paperbound. Baltimore, Maryland: Penguin Classics, 1966. 167 pp.

The translator has assembled a number of the most important diaries of Japan's great *haiku* poet, arranged them chronologically, and provided a lengthy introduction explaining the poet's work and the nature of the *haiku* in general. In these poetic diaries, which are as much interior monologues as they are travel sketches, Bashō puts himself in touch with the great traditions of Japanese poetry by visiting places known and written about by older poets. The most famous of these works is often translated "Narrow Road to the Deep North," but the other, earlier diaries, while perhaps not so profound in style or in meditative insight, are nevertheless filled with some of Bashō's most striking poetry.

The range of subject matter in these travel accounts is enormous: Japanese history, Chinese and Japanese poetry, Buddhist doctrine, aesthetics, geography, the nature of the artist, and many other topics besides, all played off against the personality of Bashō himself, who, for all his wisdom and artistic brilliance, was never too proud, or too complacent, to remain unmoved by what he saw.

Mr. Yuasa's book is invaluable because he brings all the material together in a pleasant and readable form, but—perhaps because of the difficulties in rendering the sophisticated Japanese original texts into English—the translations of the *haiku* themselves are occasionally inaccurate, and the basic form of their translation (into four lines of English) tends to reduce poetry to mere prose statement. Nevertheless the book remains the indispensable introduction to Bashō's major achievements in any Western language.

87. Matsuo Bashō. *Back Roads to Far Towns.* Tr. by Cid Corman and Kamaike Susumu. Illustrated by Hayakawa Ikutada. New York: Mushinsha/Grossman Publishers, 1968. 176 pp. (Paperback without illustrations, 146 pp.).

This adaptation of Bashō's famous *Oku no hosomichi* (The Narrow Road to the Deep North) by the American poet Cid Corman represents "imitations," to borrow Robert Lowell's term, taken to the extreme. Corman, with the assistance of Kamaike Susumu, brings all the irony and flexibility possible in contemporary poetic language to bear on Bashō's subtly crafted *haibun* and *haiku*. Although his treatment of Bashō is most unusual, the results read well and are appealing. Contrast, for example, the opening lines as rendered by Corman with those by Donald Keene.

> MOON & Sun are passing figures
> of countless generations, and years
> coming and going wanderers too.
> Drifting life away on a boat or
> meeting age leading a horse by
> the month, each day is a journey
> and the journey itself home.
>
> [P. 15]

> The months and days are the travellers of
> eternity. The years that come and go are also
> voyagers. Those who float away their lives
> on boats or who grow old leading horses
> are forever journeying, and their homes are
> wherever their travels take them.
> [Keene, *Anthology of Japanese Literature*, p. 362]

Or compare their renderings of the same *haiku*.

Corman:
> quiet
> into rock absorbing
> cicada sounds
>
> [P. 99]

Keene: Such stillness—
                          The cries of the cicadas
                          Sink into the rocks.
                                [P. 371]

In sum, Corman imposes a real style on the text—terse, colloquial, what an ideal American travel diary might turn out to be. Yet this tone may well be too dry and insufficiently elegant for those who know the magnificent Japanese of the original. Nevertheless, for those who like Corman as well as Bashō, the volume (profusely illustrated and attractively bound in the hardcover edition) is well worth a look.

88. Matsuo Bashō. "The Saga Diary." Tr. by Terasaki Etsuko. *Literature East and West* 15, no. 4 (Dec. 1971) and 16, nos. 1 and 2 (March and June 1972): 701–718.

"The Saga Diary," which describes Bashō's stay in Kyoto three years before his death, may be a less perfect work than the famous *Oku no hosomichi* (nos. **86, 87**), but the very fatigue and frailty that the text suggests draw the reader closer to Bashō's complex and beautiful human personality. Bashō discusses his reading, his visitors, his restlessness of body and mind, his nightmares over his dead disciple and friend Tokoku. All his comments seem under the spell of the atmosphere of the decaying old hut in which Bashō was living.

Perhaps one should not begin one's acquaintance with Bashō here, but when this text can be approached with the sympathy and understanding gained from a knowledge of his other diaries, "The Saga Diary" may be the most touching of all Bashō's prose works, and I am most grateful that this straightforward translation is now available.

89. Ueda Makoto. *Matsuo Bashō*. New York: Twayne Publishers, 1970. 202 pp.

Few biographies of Japanese writers have been written in any Western language, and Mr. Ueda's succinct volume is a fine beginning in what hopefully will be a long line of similar works for the well-known Twayne's World Author Series. After a short but evocative biographical sketch, Ueda proceeds to discuss in separate chapters various aspects of Bashō's literary art. In the chapter on *haiku*, Ueda traces Bashō's development. The poet began writing in the light and popular style then current but shifted to more serious poetry by experimenting with vocabulary and tone. As Mr. Ueda points out, Bashō achieved perfection in this form in his mature period. The section on *renku* (linked-verse of multiple authorship) is especially valuable, since two thirty-six poem sequences are translated in their entirety: an early example, "Winter Shower" (1684), and "Summer Moon" (1691), from the famous collection *Monkey's Raincoat* (no. **85** for another translation).

Bashō's prose diaries also receive appropriate discussion, and sample bits of *haibun* (an evocative prose style created to accompany *haiku*) are translated, some for the first time, into English. Ueda also includes a section on Bashō's aesthetics and his influence on later poets.

This biography is a sensible and appropriate place to begin for an understanding of the greatest of all Japanese poets.

90. Kobayashi Issa. *The Year of My Life.* Tr. by Yuasa Nobuyuki. Berkeley: University of California Press, 1972. 142 pp. (Paperback).

The finest Tokugawa poetic diary available in translation, outside of those of Bashō, is the charming and powerful *The Year of My Life* (*Ora ga haru*) of Kobayashi Issa (1763–1827) who, with Bashō and Buson, is considered one of the three great *haiku* poets of the period. From a simple background, and of a somewhat gentle and restrained temperament, Issa may lack the profundity of Bashō and the elegance of Buson, but the very personal flavor of his writing makes him unique.

The Year of My Life, in twenty-one short chapters, chronicles Issa's life during the year 1819. A diary in the subjective, spiritual sense, it reflects Issa's changing emotional responses to the meaning of his personal experiences. He felt a deep ambivalence to his native place, having spent years trying to escape from an extremely unpleasant stepmother. Yet he always found himself drawn back to the simple, poor beauty of the area.

GUIDE TO JAPANESE POETRY

It makes me feel
Even hotter to lie here
Looking at the mountains
I have crossed.

[P. 65]

The most moving sections of the diary deal with children and the death of Issa's own child; here, through his own art, Issa comes close to expressing what Wordsworth called "thoughts that do often lie too deep for tears."

Haïku and the *haibun* style in general are notoriously difficult to translate, and the English version by Yuasa Nobuyuki is certainly satisfactory. The book has a good introduction and a few charming illustrations.

91. MacKenzie, Lewis. *The Autumn Wind*. London: John Murray, 1957. vi, 115 pp.

Kobayashi Issa here receives his proper due in English, with a long essay on his life interspersed with translations of appropriate *haiku*.

Mr. MacKenzie has arranged his selections in several sections. "Poems of Place" takes the reader along on some of Issa's journeys and reflects the poet's enduring attachment to his native environment. The next section, "Mostly of Mid-career," shows something of the poet's moods and preoccupations during his vigorous years, and the last two sections, "Mostly in Retirement" and "Mostly of Age," chronicle Issa's work towards the end of his life.

Reading a selection of poems cannot give the unified effect of one single work, such as *The Year of My Life* (no. **90**). Yet the range of poems included is great enough that the poet's essential personality emerges. Romanized Japanese texts and necessary footnotes are provided with Mr. MacKenzie's *haiku* translations, which tend to be perhaps a bit too hearty and beef-pie British to please all American readers. However, it is an unpretentious and pleasant book on one of the great Japanese poets.

General Studies

92. Blyth, R.H. *Haiku*. 4 vols. (1, Eastern Culture; 2, Spring; 3, Summer–Autumn; 4, Autumn–Winter.) Tokyo: Hokusei-do Press, 1949–1952. xiv, 422; v, 382; xv, 443; and xiii, 396 pp.

Mr. Blyth's books on *haiku*, written with all the good humor, energy, and occasional carelessness of a true enthusiast and amateur of poetic art, may disturb the fastidious scholar, but they do present a fine and wholesome insight into Tokugawa culture, religion, and philosophy that makes their occasional shortcomings unimportant. The author's prejudices (his deep love of what he considers Zen, for example, and his determination to find comparisons between Eastern and Western poetry at every turn) may be too obvious, but the books are ultimately the stronger for them.

These four long books on *haiku*, now in their eleventh printing, are perhaps the most generally appreciated of all his works. Volume 1, Eastern Culture, deals with the spiritual origins of *haiku*, specifically Zen, and describes the social and philosophical attitudes of those poets embued with its doctrines. *Haiku* techniques are also discussed. The second volume gives examples from all periods of history of *haiku* written on subjects pertaining to spring, broken down into various elements in the aesthetic canon (mountains, festivals, birds, trees, flowers, etc.). The succeeding two volumes provide the same treatment for the other seasons.

At first the mixture of poets and periods may seem confusing, but Blyth is hoping to focus on a larger image of art and nature, of which an individual poem offers a mere glimpse. An index is provided at the end of the last volume to all poets in the four volumes, so that a poem may be traced, even if the process is a bit cumbersome.

As always in Blyth's books, each poem is given in Japanese, romanized Japanese, and English, with a commentary. The illustrations are unusual and appropriate.

93. Blyth, R.H. *A History of Haiku*. 2 vols. Tokyo: Hokuseido Press, 1964. ix, 427 and lii, 375 pp.

In these later volumes, Blyth has rearranged his material chronologically; he warns in the preface, however, that *"haiku* are not very amenable to a chronological treatment. *Haiku* are moments of vision, and the history of moments is hardly possible." Nevertheless, he makes his best efforts to stick to chronology, and he supplies a somewhat rambling commentary that gives a sense of the flow of the development of the *haiku* tradition.

The first volume goes through the works of Issa (nos. **90, 91**); the second (despite the author's announced disdain for modern *haiku*) well into the twentieth century. There is no denying the general effectiveness of the two books, but the feeling remains that Blyth prefers the sort of spiritual elbow room he provided for himself in the earlier four-volume series.

94. Brower, Gary L. *Haiku in Modern Languages: An Annotated Bibliography*. Metuchen, N.J. : Scarecrow Press, 1972. 133 pp.

This volume provides a thorough bibliography on the subject, with a surprising number of entries, often in obscure journals, of *haiku* translations, *haiku* written in English, and articles about *haiku*. Entries are provided for materials in English, Spanish, Portuguese, Italian, French, and German. An index listing names of translators and poets (including authors of *haiku* written in English and other Western languages) is also included.

A number of surprises turn up: Dag Hammarskjöld, former Secretary-General of the United Nations, wrote *haiku*, and so did the famous Greek poet George Seffris. Especially surprising is all the work being done on *haiku* in Spanish, especially in Brazil.

The brevity of the book does not permit comments by the author except for an occasional "good" or "inadequate." Carefully prepared, it is a useful book for its purpose.

95. Henderson, Harold G. *An Introduction to Haiku*. Paperbound. Garden City, New York: Doubleday Anchor Books, 1958. x, 179 pp.

Harold Henderson's delightful book on *haiku* has served as a genial introduction to the subject since its initial publication, and its popularity is easy to understand.

The plan of the book is precisely right. The opening chapter describes the characteristics of the *haiku* form: its suggestiveness, its brevity, the special vocabulary of *kigo* ("season words") and *kireji* ("cutting words"). A fine appendix of *kireji*, with concise and practical definitions, is included.

The author then describes the history of *haiku* from the early poets through Bashō to Buson, Issa, and Shiki. He includes biographical information and historical background in combination with generous translations of *haiku*; he provides, in addition to his polished English rendering, a literal word-for-word English translation and the Japanese text in romanized letters. A student who knows some Japanese can study the translation process in sufficient detail so that the book, like Arthur Waley's *The Uta* (no. **60**), can serve as an excellent means of training for translation. The book is primarily intended, however, for those who read *haiku* in English.

The one unusual feature of the book is Mr. Henderson's decision to rhyme his translations. The results are sometimes effective, but the temptation to match rhymes often forces a somewhat superficial quality into serious poetry that threatens to turn some of them into the very "epigrams" that Henderson stoutly (and rightly) insists they are not.

For example, compare Henderson's rendering of Bashō

> Won't you come and see
> Loneliness? Just one leaf
> From the *kiri* tree.
> [P. 47]

with that of R. H. Blyth:

> A paulownia leaf has fallen;
> Will you not visit
> My loneliness?
> [*Haiku*, vol. 4, p. 130]

Blyth's version carries the weight and dignity worthy of the sentiment being expressed precisely because of the lack of rhyme. The book nevertheless is highly recommended.

96. Henderson, Harold. *Haiku in English*. Paperbound. Rutland and Tokyo: Charles E. Tuttle Co., 1967. 44 pp.

This slender book, not much more than a pamphlet, is concerned primarily with the composition of *haiku* in English rather than with Japanese *haiku* as such; nevertheless, Henderson's explanations provide considerable insight into the composition of the Japanese poems that are given as examples. The book is an important source for those interested in the structure of the verse form in either language.

97. Kanaseki Hisao. "Haiku and Modern American Poetry." *The East–West Review* 3, no. 3 (Winter 1967–68): 223–41.

This urbane and most observant essay deals with what modern American poets interested in the form have *not* properly understood. It is highly recommended as an antidote to too many cherry blossoms, in either language.

98. Miyamori Asatarō. *An Anthology of Haiku Ancient and Modern*. (1932). Westport, Connecticut: Greenwood Press, 1971. xxiv, 841 pp.

Venerable texts on Japanese literature must be approached with certain apprehension, but a look at Mr. Miyamori's book should bring surprise and considerable delight to the reader who seeks some detail on the history of *haiku*. The history of the form is sketched out in an essay of a hundred pages, beginning with the period prior to the work of Bashō and going up through Masaoka Shiki (see also nos. **110**, **111**) and his contemporaries in the early twentieth century. Then follows a voluminous collection of *haiku* by all the great masters, with texts in Japanese, roman letters, translations, and commentaries on the fuller meanings of the poems. The translations themselves are often somewhat pedestrian because of the Victorian language used, but they are usually clear: the poems can be grasped at least linguistically and intellectually. One particularly valuable feature is the inclusion of alternate translations by other Japanese or Western scholars of many of the more important *haiku*, thus offering the reader the experience of coming to grips with the various dimensions of a single good *haiku*.

The sheer diversity of material gives the book a unique value. There are quantities of (often good) poems by secondary poets otherwise unavailable in English; in the modern period alone, more than seventy *haiku* by Shiki are included, as well as a considerable number by Natsume Sōseki (1867–1916), greatest of the modern Japanese novelists, who wrote poetry early in his career.

Despite its occasional shortcomings in fluency of translation, this is a fine compendium. A number of appropriate illustrations enhance the text.

99. Nippon Gakujutsu Shinkōkai. *Haikai and Haiku*. Tokyo: Nippon Gakujutsu Shinkōkai, 1958. xxv, 191 pp.

The poetics of *haiku* and *haikai* (linked-verse composed of *haiku* elements) are very complex, and this readable yet scholarly book is an altogether indispensable introduction to the subject. The volume was compiled by a number of noted Japanese experts in the field, then translated into English by several British scholars.

The book treats *haiku* by period, chronicling the work of the best poets. Background information, translations, and commentaries are provided. A number of poets of some distinction included here are not otherwise readily found in English; one longer work of Buson, "Lines on the Kema Banks in the Spring Breeze," is of first importance and unavailable elsewhere.

Even more valuable, however, are the biographies of the poets and a series of notes on the aesthetics of *haiku*. Students of Japanese literature who have wrestled with such difficult terms as *yūgen, shibumi, sabi,* and *hosomi* can find here, if not answers to their questions, at least exceedingly intelligent assistance.

An effective discussion and listing of the so-called *kigo* or season words are also provided.

The book is beautifully printed and is graced with a number of unusual illustrations, including Bashō's diagram of a snore! For the serious reader this is an essential book, for pleasure and for reference.

100. Wilson, William Ritchie. "The Truth of *haikai.*" Monumenta Nipponica 26, nos. 1–2 (1971): 49–53.

Notes on poetic practice at the time of Bashō, taken from collections on the aesthetics of *haikai* and *haiku* written by his disciples, are translated, with a commentary, by Mr. Wilson. The article can serve as a supplement to excerpts from the same collections in *Sources of the Japanese Tradition* (no. 8).

101. Yasuda, Kenneth. *The Japanese Haiku.* Rutland, Vermont, and Tokyo: Charles E. Tuttle Co., 1957. xx, 232 pages. (Paperback).

"Any work of art," writes the author, "can be enjoyed through an act of immediate perception, without conscious effort or reasoning," and he then proceeds to compare Western poems —by Amy Lowell, Ezra Pound, William Carlos Williams and others—with the work of the great *haiku* poets in order to reveal some of the same principles at work. His grasp of Western literature, plus his sense of what an English-speaking reader, nurtured on English and American poetry, needs to know to appreciate the form, makes his arguments persuasive. The sections on aesthetic experience, the relationship between form and content in *haiku*, and the rhythms of *haiku* imagery are the most extended and useful treatment of these subjects now available in English.

Mr. Yasuda is also interested in the problems of translating *haiku* into English and composing them in English, and certain portions of the book take up these questions of more specialized concern. Nevertheless, a reader seeking insight into the nature of *haiku* will find these discussions of interest as well, since they contain explanations about the nature of poetic statement in both languages.

Some historical material is included, as well as sample translations of *haiku* by the great masters of the form. Basically, however, this is a book on technique—developing it, appreciating it—and as such has remained unsurpassed since its publication.

102. Matsumoto Shigeru. *Motoori Norinaga.* Cambridge: Harvard University Press, 1970. viii, 201 pp.

This study of the famous eighteenth-century literary critic and student of early Japanese religion is not a book about poetry at all, but by using the index, the reader will be able to glean information about *waka* theory and practice during the Tokugawa period, a subject unaccountably left out of most books on the history of Japanese literature. Motoori was an accomplished poet and participated in the literary debates of the day.

103. Ōkuma Kotomichi. A *Grass Path: Selected Poems from the "Sōkeishū."* Tr. by Uyehara Yukuo and Marjorie Sinclair. Honolulu: University of Hawaii Press, 1955. xvi, 73 pp.

Recognizing change within tradition is one of the real pleasures available to those who enjoy reading poetry, and this collection of *waka* by Ōkuma Kotomichi (1798–1868) is a fine example of a venerable poetic form infused with a new spirit.

Waka had its first great flowering in the Heian period; the poems were written by the aristocracy, for the aristocracy. Later, in the Tokugawa period, commoners learned the rules of the form and *waka* became, within modest limits, a popular art form. The democratization of poetry, unfortunately, also brought mediocrity and blandness. Kotomichi, who died on the eve of the Meiji Restoration, brought new insights to his poetry that are more suggestive of the forward-looking Meiji period that followed than of the end of the Tokugawa. In his critical writing he spoke of the poetic response of the writer himself as the only sure inspiration for a proper poem, not any adherence to a preordained subject. He insisted that a poet must write simply and naturally.

Kotomichi had a fine eye.

> Rain in spring,
> Gentle, mistlike:
> Before reaching the earth,
> The drops are lost.
>
> [P. 17]

His humor and humanity too provide an attractive element in the poems translated here.

> Look! Already I carry
> My hands behind me and stoop—
> An old man.
> From whom and when, I wonder,
> Did I learn this gesture?
>
> [P. 2]

The translations in this little book are unpretentious and sufficiently accurate to give a clear impression of the poet's mind and art. Altogether, it is a very satisfying volume and provides the only translations available of an important poet.

Chinese Poetry

104. Kodama Misao, and Yanagishima Hikosaku. *Ryōkan the Great Fool.* Kyoto: Kyoto Seika Junior College Press, 1969. 112 pp.

The Tokugawa period saw the composition of poetry in various styles. Some of the greatest was in the Chinese language. So far, however, little of this verse, often of a philosophic or a religious nature, has attracted the attention of Western translators, despite its high quality.

This earnest little book attempts to introduce the work of Ryōkan (1758–1831), a Buddhist monk and recluse who was a major figure in Tokugawa poetry. His life and work have come to be highly appreciated in contemporary Japan; indeed, Kawabata Yasunari expressed his admiration for Ryōkan in his 1968 Nobel Prize speech (no. **28**).

Unfortunately these translations will not win any converts to his work. The valiant efforts made to render these sophisticated and philosophically profound poems (mostly originally in Chinese, a few in Japanese) have failed because of faulty English. The book has not been carefully edited, adding confusion to obscurity.

Nevertheless, the volume does give biographical information and the texts (in the original and in translation) of a number of important poems, both in Chinese and Japanese. From them, Ryōkan's Zen experience emerges clearly.

> What can I compare
> The world to?
> Isn't it as void and empty
> As an echo dying away?
> [P. 75]

His human qualities are revealed as well.

> How can I tell the floating world
> The penetrating loneliness of a man
> Living in a solitary hut all by himself
> During the long, silent winter night?
> [P. 28]

A few scattered poems of Ryōkan have been translated elsewhere, but he still awaits his proper introduction in a Western language. The present book, admirable in purpose, only serves to whet the appetite.

Comic Verse

105. Blyth, R.H. *Japanese Life and Character in Senryū*. Tokyo: Hokuseido Press, 1961. viii, 628 pp.
106. ———. *Edo Satirical Verse Anthologies*. Tokyo: Hokuseido Press, 1961. 312 pp.

"I feel that the fundamental thing in the Japanese character is a peculiar combination of poetry and humor. 'Poetry' means the ability to see, to know by intuition what is interesting, what is really valuable in things and persons. 'Humor' means the joyful, unsentimental pathos that arises from the paradox inherent in the nature of things." With this premise, R.H. Blyth has compiled a voluminous and stimulating treatise on the comic Tokugawa verse called *senryū*, the subject matter of which he defines as "the other half that *haiku* omits."

Blyth begins with a lengthy historical survey of the form from the 1580s to the early twentieth century, outlining the work of major authors and discussing the chief poetry collections. He gives many trenchant examples, and surprisingly, some of the modern *senryū* are the most striking.

To ease the patient's mind,	Looking suspicious,
The doctor changes	He looks
The color of the medicine.	Suspicious-looking.
[By Tojibō, p. 190]	[By Garyūbō, p. 189]

Blyth then breaks down his subject into various categories he finds appropriate—psychology, women, animals, and so forth—and provides examples from each period. One chapter of particular interest is that entitled "Unconsidered Trifles," "those small but deeply significant matters that show us some absolute value in the most trivial thing."

At the telephone,	The found ring;
They laugh	The policeman
Alternately.	Tries it on his finger.
[By Shisambō, p. 293]	[By Tonsui, p. 295]

The chapter on the "Humour of *Senryu*" provides examples of Grim Humour, Irony, Tragic Humour, Shakespearian Humour, Indirect Humour, and a number of others in Blyth-like categories. The professions—doctors, teachers, etc.—are also dealt with. *Senryū* that draw on Chinese and Japanese history are discussed, as well as genre poems and Buddhist verses. The last two chapters treat poetic style and philosophy in *senryū*. Appended at the end of the book are four groups of *senryū* arranged by the seasons and a short article on two poets who helped keep the form alive in modern times, Inoue Kenkabō (1870–1934), and Sakai Kuraki (1869–1942).

The book should by no means be considered a mere catalogue. It is a fine, lengthy potpourri well worthy of its subject. The poems in translation are almost invariously humorous, at least in that special sense of the word used by Blyth. His commentaries on the poems (given in both Japanese and *rōmaji* with the English version) are always helpful. The author knew Western literature in general and English literature in particular very well (before his death in 1964, he taught English and English literature in Japan) and his comments are larded with thought-provoking references to Emily Dickinson, Wordsworth, Pope, French philosophers, Chinese mystics, and a host of other important figures in world culture.

In his subsequent *Edo Satirical Verse Anthologies*, Blyth translates examples from a number of the most important anthologies, especially the *Mutamagawa* (Mutama River), edited by Keikiitsu (1694–1761), which was published over a period of twenty-six years, from 1750 to 1776. Also included are a number of excerpts from the [*Haifū*] *Yanagidaru* (A Willow Barrelful of Light Verse), published in 167 volumes between 1765 and 1837. The first volumes in this extensive collection, incidentally, were edited by the critic Karai Senryū (1718–1790). Although he was not a poet in his own right, his reputation as an editor was so great that these humorous verses came to be called by his name. (Originally they were humorous *haiku* or parts of a *renga* sequence.)

Edo Satirical Verse Anthologies also contains brief excerpts from several other less important collections.

Again, the translations are alert and attractive, and Japanese and *rōmaji* texts are provided. As always, the humor is surprisingly modern, and surprisingly humane.

> It is unbecoming
> To be scolded
> Now that I am thirty-nine.
> [P. 149]

This is a fine companion volume to *Japanese Life and Character in Senryū*, and little material is duplicated.

107. Blyth, R. H. *Oriental Humor*. Tokyo: Hokuseido Press, 1959. 582 pp.

Strictly speaking, Mr. Blyth's compendium is not a book on poetry at all, but a rambling, and generally quite entertaining, discussion of humor in China, Korea, and Japan. Poetry comes in for extended treatment, however, and a judicious use of the index will turn up considerable information on *haiku*, *senryū*, and virtually the only information available in English on *kyōka*, or humorous *waka*.

VIII. The Modern Period (1868–present)
Waka

108. Ishikawa Takuboku. *Poems to Eat.* Tr. by Carl Sesar. Tokyo and Palo Alto: Kodansha International, 1966. 168 pp.

These brilliant translations by Carl Sesar offer a series of 159 *waka* by Ishikawa Takuboku (1885–1912), one of the great geniuses of modern Japanese literature. Takuboku, who came from a humble background, tried hard to make his way in the world and died, struggling with tuberculosis, at the age of twenty-six. He wrote with great mastery in every form he attempted, but these *waka* may represent, along with his extraordinary *Rōmaji Diary* (available in a complete translation by Donald Keene in his anthology *Modern Japanese Literature*, no. **124**) his most striking accomplishments. *Waka* had traditionally been severely restricted in vocabulary and subject matter, but Takuboku expanded its definitions. "I got the idea for the title 'Poems to Eat,' " he wrote, "from a beer advertisement I often saw in the streetcar. I mean by it poems that are down to earth, poems with feelings unremoved from real life. Not delicacies, not a feast, but poems that taste like our daily meals; poems, then, that are *necessities* to us." This fresh attitude resulted in radical *waka* and very accomplished modern poetry. Takuboku's sense of himself is never absent from these intensely personal, often ironic vignettes of a soul in search of his universe: the paradigm of modern man.

Carl Sesar's translations, although often somewhat freely adapted from the original, strike precisely the right tone; altogether, this book, with its effective woodcut illustrations by Kuwata Masakazu, is one of the finest translations of any Japanese poetry available in English.

109. Yosano Akiko. *Tangled Hair: Selected Tanka from "Midaregami."* Tr. by Sanford Goldstein and Shinoda Seishi. Lafayette: Purdue University Studies, 1971. xi, 164 pp.

Tanka, the standard form of Japanese poetry since Heian times, fell into comparative disfavor in the Meiji period, when new themes, new emotions called for a verse form powerful enough to encompass them. A number of young writers tried to reform the now-genteel *tanka*, however, to make it a suitable vehicle for contemporary poetry, and in this effort no one was more effective than Yosano Akiko (1878–1941), whose husband, Yosano Tekkan, was also a poet. She used her poems as a means of keeping a diary of her tangled and vibrant emotional relationships. Her first published collection, *Tangled Hair* (1901), caused a sensation among those accustomed to the traditional boundaries of diction and subject matter.

Sanford Goldstein and Shinoda Seishi's translations manage to convey a good sense of the urgency and passion these short poems can evoke:

Incense smoke	So that poem was only
Curling up round	For diversion
The hair of my departed friend,	While you drank?
Hair that I envied	Well, you cross it out!
When she was alive.	I can't!
[No. 61]	[No. 138]

One must go back to the woman court poet of the Heian period, Ono no Komachi (see no. **51**), for *tanka* of similar personal intensity.

The book is a model of its kind. The authors have provided a lengthy introduction, outlining the background of Akiko's accomplishments and some details of her personal life, necessary for an understanding of this highly personal poetry. In addition, there are texts in Japanese and *rōmaji* as well as discreet and thoughtful notes on each individual poem.

110. Brower, Robert. "Masaoka Shiki and Tanka Reform." In *Tradition and Modernization in Japanese Culture*, ed. by Donald Shively. pp. 379–418. Princeton: Princeton University Press, 1971.

Brower provides a lengthy account of Shiki's life, critical writing, and artistic accomplishments. The result is a fascinating re-creation of both the poet and the complex period in which he lived. The article is on the whole the most reliable and sympathetic account of Shiki in a Western language.

Haiku

111. Masaoka Shiki. *Peonies Kana. A Selection of Haiku.* Tr. by
     Harold J. Isaacson. Paperbound. New York: Theatre Arts
     Books, 1972. xxvii, 89 pp.

Masaoka Shiki (1867–1902), the finest modern poet who wrote
in the traditional forms of *waka* and *haiku,* has been the subject
of perceptive essays written by Donald Keene in *Landscapes
and Portraits* (no. **23**) and Robert Brower in *Tradition and Moderni-
zation in Japanese Culture* (no. **110**). Isaacson, however, gives
us for the first time a volume dedicated to translations of a
considerable number of Shiki's own poems. The translations
will not please everyone. Isaacson leaves in the Japanese parti-
cles so important for setting up the major juxtapositions in a
haiku. Combined with his informal diction, the results are some-
times artificial, even ambiguous.

> That the moon would show—
> a lie ya As a matter of fact
> icy shower kana
> [P. 30]

On the other hand, some of the translations seem breathtak-
ingly right:

> Late afternoon downpour;
> when it had ended along came
> somebody selling young trees.
> [P. 26]

There is an introduction that is, alas, not notable for the kind
of insights a reader might hope for. Isaacson insists that "these
haiku are all of high perfection," yet they often seem merely
pretty, where Bashō, even Buson, are strong. Some comparisions
with these or other poets to show Shiki's particular affinities
and accomplishments in the form would have been in order,
and much more useful than the inclusion of a translation of
Tōgan koji, a *nō* play attributed to Zeami. Effective as it is,
it has ultimately little to do with Shiki's art.

Neither Japanese nor romanized texts are included. There is a good glossary and an index of poems by season.

112. Ueda Makoto. *Modern Japanese Haiku: An Anthology*. Toronto, Canada: University of Toronto Press, 1975. vii, 265 pp.

"When we think of Japanese *haiku*, we usually think of the works of old masters like Bashō, Buson, and Issa." Mr. Ueda follows his opening statement with a lucid introduction to the developments and accomplishments in the *haiku* form during the late nineteenth and twentieth centuries, a hitherto woefully neglected subject for study by foreign scholars. He discusses the reforms of Masaoka Shiki (see nos. **110, 111**), who began the movement for modern *haiku*, and chronicles the activities of various groups and individual poets up to the present day. The anthology itself, which forms the bulk of the volume, consists of poetry translations by twenty-five poets, followed by brief but most informative biographical sketches of each writer.

Ueda's assessment of modern *haiku* clearly reveals that the form is far more flexible and powerful than its present-day detractors would have us believe. If any quality serves to differentiate modern *haiku* from those of earlier periods, it is the new emphasis on thrusting the poet's personality directly into the poem. The resulting subjective force is evident, even in the work of Masaoka Shiki (1867–1902).

> New Year's calendar:
>   in the month of May, there is
>   a day for my death.

Some of the postwar *haiku* breaks the traditional rules, yet the total effect is, by the new and expanded definitions given *haiku* in the modern period, powerful and apposite to the form, as can be illustrated by this poem by Kaneko Tōta (b. 1910).

> After a heated argument
>   I go out to the street
>   and become a motorcycle.

Haiku by such noted novelists as Akutagawa Ryūnosuke (1892–1927) and Natsume Sōseki (1867–1916) introduce us to another facet of the art of these men who concerned themselves with the interplay of personality and incident in their prose writing; their *haiku* bring the personality of the poets closer to the surface. Here is one of Akutagawa's poems.

> The day autumn began
> I had a cavity in my tooth
> filled with silver.

Ueda's translations are smooth, and he aids the reader by providing both the Japanese text in roman letters and a literal translation of the text.

The volume does more than merely fill a gap in the reader's understanding of an ongoing art form; we are given the chance to discover and enjoy a body of subtle and moving poetry until now unavailable in English.

Chinese Poetry

113. Natsume Sōseki. "Sixteen Chinese Poems by Natsume Sōseki," tr. by Burton Watson. In *Essays on Natsume Sōseki's Works,* ed. by Japanese National Commission for UNESCO. pp. 119–24. Tokyo: Japan Society for the Promotion of Science, 1970.

Natsume Sōseki (1867–1917), the great novelist of modern Japan, was a fine poet in the style of Chinese verse favored by Tokugawa artists and scholars. Burton Watson gives us a sample of Sōseki's extremely personal and moving poems through his beautiful translations. One can only wish that he had gone on to render many more in English.

Free Verse

114. Hagiwara Sakutarō. *Face at the Bottom of the World and other Poems.* Tr. by Graeme Wilson. Rutland, Vermont: Charles E. Tuttle Co., 1969. 83 pp.

Japanese modern poetry of the highest caliber can be said to have begun with the work of Hagiwara Sakutarō (1886–1942) when he published his collection *Tsuki ni hoeru* (Barking at the Moon) in 1917. Nishiwaki Junzaburō, the finest poet of the early postwar years, was in Europe at the time, learning to write in French and English; when he read Hagiwara, he wrote, "he has shown me that modern poetry can be created in our own language," and began his own proper career.

Hagiwara's value far exceeds that of a mere literary model. He was often referred to as a Japanese Rimbaud, and his bohemian and slightly sour life was brilliantly caught in the lyrical vision he produced. His language was colloquial, and he solved the problem of poetic organization in modern Japanese by resource to symbols that unite and give resonance to long passages of verse. The fact that he may have learned this from reading the French symbolists is far less important than the fact that he made these techniques his own.

Graeme Wilson has chosen forty of Hagiwara's poems for translation, which provide a certain sense of the poet's vision. Translations rarely suit every reader's taste, and several aspects of the book are disappointing. The translation of one full collection, rather than scattered poems, would have given a much better sense of the architecture of Hagiwara's poetry, because symbols, colors, images, objects move from poem to poem, recast and reshaped to a strength of necessity invisible in one or two poems. Also, the use of rhyme, although defended by Wilson, is confining—rather like putting a carefully trimmed hedge around a seething whirlpool. Nevertheless, Wilson's dexterity with the English language has resulted in a number of effectively terse and intelligible poems that can be directly enjoyed by the English-speaking reader.

The book has a well-wrought and fairly comprehensive introduction, and the book includes some abstract illustrations and a photograph of the poet.

115. Kusano Shimpei. *Frogs & Others.* Tr. by Cid Corman. New York: Mushinsha/Grossman Publishers, 1969. 124 pp.

Kusano Shimpei (b. 1903) was one of the first poets in Japan to champion the work of Miyazawa Kenji; now he, like the

legendary figure he helped to popularize, has caught the atten-
tion of younger American poets, who are perhaps attracted both
by Kusano's splendid sense of humor and by his deep and
fundamental relationship to the natural world.

In 1968 Cid Corman made selections from Kusano's works,
including a short anthology *Frogs*, choosing poems that he per-
sonally found appealing. The results are altogether striking: Cor-
man's free and ironic use of the English language, plus his
unerring sense of the tonal value of words and his ability to
create conglomerations of sounds, makes some of these English
renderings as vibrant in their own way as Ezra Pound's transla-
tions from the ancient Chinese *Book of Songs*. In fact, these
translations may suffer from what to some readers will appear
as an inevitable defect: they are actually re-creations of the Japa-
nese originals. The contemporary climate in American poetry
permits Corman a more mordant, involved, and occasionally
flippant language than the original Japanese suggests. Neverthe-
less, the results are fine poetry, and the special sense of depth
without sentimentality in Kusano's work is beautifully con-
veyed.

The book is elaborately designed, one of the most attractive
in the generally excellent Mushinsha series.

116. Miyazawa Kenji. Poems translated by Gary Snyder in his
     collection *The Back Country*. New York: New Directions,
     1968. 128 pp. (Paperback).
117. ———. *Spring & Asura*. Tr. by Sato Hiroaki. Chicago:
     Chicago Review Press, 1973. 104 pp. (Paperback).

Miyazawa Kenji (1896–1933) had an unusual career as a poet.
Born in a northern rural area, he studied farming and taught
at an agricultural school; he became a Nichiren Buddhist and
dedicated his professional career to teaching agrarian methodol-
ogy to the sons of uneducated farmers. And he wrote poetry,
filled with complex allusions to Buddhism, nature, and modern
scientific thought.

Miyazawa's dedication to the realities of common life and
his indifference to the literary world of his time attracted a
number of admirers, among them Kusano Shimpei (no. **115**),
who helped collect and edit Miyazawa's work after his death.

In recent years Miyazawa has gained foreign admirers for many of the same reasons. Among them is the American poet Gary Snyder, who translated eighteen of Miyazawa's poems in his book *The Back Country*. Snyder's English versions are as satisfying as his own original work, yet faithful, both in language and intention, to the original Japanese. The effect is a kind of homage from the younger poet to the elder. The poems he chose to translate are largely scenic descriptions that in turn serve as screens through which one glimpses the ineffable, great forces of nature—images of trees, clouds, forests caught in great movements of light, space, and time. Juxtaposed with these visions are several poems showing Miyazawa as a cool-headed and humane observer of the society he saw around him.

A fuller view of Miyazawa's work can be gained by reading the book-length collection of translations by the gifted Sato Hiroaki. Over seventy poems are included, some of them quite long. Sato's English style may be somewhat less individual than Snyder's, but it is wonderfully flexible, and Sato is fully able to make Miyazawa a poet in English. Here are the four lines of the poem "Sapporo City:"

> The gray light avalanched in the distance.
> Over the sand of the distorted square
> I scattered sorrows like blue myths
> but the birds would not touch them.
>
> [P. 69]

Half a dozen poems translated by Snyder are also found in Sato's book, and a comparison provides double glosses by these two gifted writers on some of the most arresting poetry in the modern period. Sato's volume also includes a fine introduction by Burton Watson of Columbia University which gives a straightforward and useful biographical account of Miyazawa that helps to set him in his time and place, although he cannot be contained there.

118. Shimazaki Tōson. Translations and commentaries on his poems by James R. Morita in "Shimazaki Tōson's Four Collections of Poems." *Monumenta Nipponica* 25, nos. 3–4 (1970): 325–69.

Literary histories usually list Shimazaki Tōson (1872–1943) as the creator of the first original modern poems in Japanese. They are found in his 1897 anthology *Wakanashū* (Seedlings). Tōson later turned to prose, writing a number of highly personal novels, several of which are landmarks in modern Japanese fiction. These romantic poems of his youth, however, continue to hold their high reputation and are always found in standard Japanese-language anthologies of modern verse.

The article provides important historical background, but the translations are disappointing. Stripped of the sounds and rhythms of the originals, these poems, reduced to their contents, alternate between the tedious, the obscure, and the exasperating. Tōson's poems are said to have struck Japanese readers at the time of their publication with great freshness, but in English they only cloy.

119. Takagi Kyōzō. *Selected Poems.* Tr. by James Kirkup and Nakano Michio. Cheadle, Cheshire, England: Carcanet Press, 1973. 51 pp.

This attractive, small volume serves as a proper first introduction to the work of Takagi Kyōzō (b. 1903), one of the few modern Japanese poets to compose in his local dialect, a northern version of the language considerably different, the translators tell us, from standard Tokyo speech. Takagi's reputation extends beyond his use of dialect, however, and so even in standard English the poems are striking.

> The sun glares.
> The road is white.
> The clouds are gradually coming to the boil.
> The wind is already chill.
> Along the concrete wall
> My shadow goes crawling.
> I find an exhausted butterfly in my path.
>
> In this scene turned inside out,
> I shall walk like an evangelist
> Listening to faint, far-off thunders.
> ["Day of Metamorphosis," p. 38]

Takagi's verse is sparse, colloquial, and removed from the foreign, largely intellectual, influences that helped form the sophisticated art of his contemporaries, Hagiwara Sakutarō and Nishiwaki Junzaburō. In a simple and affecting autobiographical note, Takagi mentions that he read T.S. Eliot when he was well into his fifties, only after Nishiwaki published his famous translation of *The Wasteland*. Takagi's work sometimes suggests the brevity and profundity of traditional Japanese verse. For example, his poem "Knife"

> In a stony place
> grasshoppers were chirping.
> I got a pain in my forehead.
> [P. 25]

is reminiscent of the effect obtained in Bashō's great *haiku*:

> The silence;
> The voice of the cicadas
> Penetrates the rocks.
> [Blyth, *Haiku*, vol. 3, p. 229]

Takagi, like Takahashi Shinkichi (no. **120**), the Zen poet, remains somewhat outside the mainstream of the Tokyo-centered Japanese literary world, and the English reader is fortunate that enthusiastic translators have sought such men out and made their work available.

120. Takahashi Shinkichi. *Afterimages: Zen Poems*. Tr. by Lucien Stryk and Ikemoto Takashi. Paperbound. New York: Doubleday Anchor Books, 1972. xv, 137 pp.

Takahashi (b. 1901) is a self-educated man; his considerable knowledge of Eastern and Western literature was a result of his own searching and personal experience. He wrote the first poetry in the *dada* style in Japan in the 1920s, then, in 1928, undertook the serious study of Zen. His poetry reflects both interests. The connections between the two seem, to some extent, apparent: strange juxtapositions, shiftings of time and space, and the mocking of values—inherited culture in the case of *dada*, illusions of the self in the case of Zen.

Lucien Stryk and Ikemoto Takashi selected ninety poems from the writer's later collections, omitting the early work altogether. The poems included in *Afterimages* require a reader who is not afraid to scrutinize the text carefully and yet who does not suffer from anything remotely resembling a literal mind. One of the fascinating aspects of Takahashi's work is the close relation it bears to the kind of free association associated in the West with the most advanced modern poetry, while at the same time maintaining close links with the great Zen poetry tradition of the past. One is often reminded of the mystic verses of the T'ang dynasty Chinese monk Han Shan (see, for example, the excellent translations made by Burton Watson in *Cold Mountain*, Columbia University Press, 1970).

Stryk's translations (cf. nos. **81, 82**) often permit the reader to see beyond the words themselves towards the giant images moving behind the poet's individual expression of them.

> Standing with cold bare feet
> Atop the universe,
> Raking down the ashes of logic,
> My voice will be fresh again.
> [Excerpt from p. 129]

The translators have provided a fine setting for the poems. Biographical material is added, all pertinent to the poetry, and Stryk has included a beautifully crafted essay on Zen poetics. He leads the reader—often by means of judicious use of Western comparisons—closer to a grasp of the essential atmosphere in which the poems must be read.

Anthologies

121. Bownas, Geoffrey, and Mishima Yukio. *New Writing in Japan*. Paperbound. Baltimore, Maryland: Penguin Books, 1972. 249 pp.

One of the newest Penguin anthologies, this volume is edited by Geoffrey Bownas, one of the editors of *The Penguin Book of Japanese Verse* (no. **14**), and Mishima Yukio, the well-known Japanese novelist who committed suicide in 1972. They selected a group of prominent writers whose work "came fairly and squarely within the scope of our definition of 'contemporary Japan.' " Their definition does not include authors with politically leftist orientations, so a number of the most important figures in the field of postwar poetry are not represented. Much of the book is made up of prose selections, but nine poets are included, with forty-odd pages dedicated to their work. Several of these—Anzai Hitoshi, Tanikawa Shuntarō, and Shiraishi Kazuko—are well known through other translations, but several of the others, equally worth reading, are new to the English-language public. The English versions, by Mr. Bownas and the gifted English poet James Kirkup, both of whom have lived in Japan, are effective, but as is usually the case with these collections, we are given only frustrating glimpses of the poets. Takahashi Mutsuo (a kind of Japanese Frank O'Hara) writes erotic and elegant verse but there is too little included here to give any clear picture of his world; Tamura Ryūichi, one of the most distinguished of the postwar poets, is represented by only two poems, both so simple and so masterful that the reader is disappointed when he turns the page and finds no more.

Most of the poetry translated is in the modern style, but there are five experimental *tanka* by Tsukamoto Kunio and a group of contemporary *haiku* by Mizushima Hatsu.

Although a good introduction to new poetry in Japan, proper acquaintance is not possible in so short a space.

122. Fitzsimmons, Thomas. *Japanese Poetry Now*. London: Rapp and Whiting, 1972. 134 pp.

As the title page states, Mr. Fitzsimmons, himself a poet, has "remade" the poetry here translated into English. He has not hesitated to reshape and reword his originals, although he has done so with the help of several Japanese poets, Gary Snyder, and a variety of Japanese scholars of modern literature. His experiments include placement of lines on the page, vertical typography, and special capitalizations to space and break his lines. Such methods produce a tone appropriate for much of the poetry in this book.

Many younger poets well known in Japan but unavailable in English are represented in this volume, each by a few transla-tions. Fitzsimmons has included a number of "new left" writers whose work forms such an important part of the Japanese post-war literary scene. Tanikawa Shuntarō and Ōka Makoto (his poem of the death of Marilyn Monroe shows something of the complexities of the contemporary scene) read especially well here, and a few older poets, such as the splendid Takami Jun (1907–1965), are finally given sufficient space in an anthology to permit the reader to gain some sense of the quality of their poetry.

There remains, however, a certain similarity of diction in all these poems, "remade" as they are by a single writer whose language is more informal, and occasionally more violent, than that of the original poets. For this reason, these translations are probably best enjoyed a few at a time.

123. Guest, Harry; Guest, Lynn; and Kajima Shōzō, eds. *Post-War Japanese Poetry*. Paperbound. Baltimore, Maryland: Penguin Books, 1972. 165 pp.

A good selection of contemporary poems has been translated by Harry Guest, an English poet of some reputation. The transla-tions are colloquial, as usually befit the originals, and the exper-iments with typography, designed to transmit the effect of the original poems into English, are usually quite successful. The work of several good poets not otherwise available in translation is welcome, including the concrete poetry by Niikuni Seiichi. The only complaint is the typical one of any reader—too few pages for too many poets, over forty of them.

A thought-provoking introduction, with some first-rate obser-vations on the techniques of modern poetry and the special qualities of the Japanese language, is well worth careful reading, and the brief biographical sketches of the poets usually relate to the poems that follow—a refreshing contribution in itself.

124. Keene, Donald, ed. *Modern Japanese Literature*. New York: Grove Press, 1956. 440 pp. (Paperback).

Since its appearance, this anthology has remained the standard collection of English translations of prose and poetry written in Japan since 1868. In many ways this collection has been superceded, as new prose translations can be obtained elsewhere, but for modern poetry, there are a number of items of great literary merit not otherwise available.

Chief among them is the extraordinary *Rōmaji Diary* of Ishikawa Takuboku (cf. no. **108**), an intimate chronicle of the feelings and reactions of one of Japan's great modern poets. The diary was written over a period of several months in 1909. Most of the text is in prose, but some poetry is interspersed. Takuboku permits a glimpse into his spiritual state, his doubts, his ambitions, his own view of his hypocrisies, and his disappointments. The *Rōmaji Diary* is one of the most moving documents in modern Japanese literature, and the anthology is worth obtaining for that text alone.

In addition, the anthology contains poetry by such respected modern poets as Shimazaki Tōson (no. **118**), Yosano Akiko (no. **109**), Hagiwara Sakutarō (no. **114**), and Takuboku himself. Modern *waka* and *haiku* are included, and there is even a section on poetry written in Chinese, that last artistic legacy of the Tokugawa period to the late nineteenth century. Among these is a charming description of Niagara Falls that might have been composed by a T'ang poet.

All the poetry translations (many by Keene himself) are highly satisfactory and, read together, provide a brief but successful introduction to the range of modern poetry written in Japan.

125. Kijima Hajime, ed. *The Poetry of Postwar Japan.* Iowa City: University of Iowa Press, forthcoming, 1975. 324 pp.

This anthology (read in manuscript) promises to be one of the most comprehensive and stimulating selections of contemporary Japanese poetry yet to appear in any Western language. The editor has included over thirty writers (roughly as many as in the Guest *Post-War Japanese Poetry,* no. **123**), but offers in most cases a representative selection of their work. The highly respected poets—Tamura Ryūichi, Tanikawa Shuntarō, and one

or two others—receive considerable space, usually without du-
plicating poetry translated elsewhere. In addition, the reader
can extend his acquaintance to such striking talents as Ōka
Makoto, Iwata Hiroshi, and Hasegawa Shiro. Iwata's almost
surrealist humor, Hasegawa's Brecht-inspired social commen-
taries, Ōka's elegant images, and Kuroda Kio's political posters
are only part of the incredible diversity found in the book.
A generous and impressive selection of poems by Kijima himself
is also included: an emphasis on jazz makes them fully contem-
porary, altogether international.

A number of gifted translators have worked on the collection.
There is a special pleasure for the reader in the fact that often
several translators have worked on the same poet. The differ-
ences in their style most effectively reveal the nature of the
poet.

The general impression gained from the anthology is that
poetry has been politicized in postwar Japan. The war, Hiro-
shima, Vietnam, radical student protest: these are the realities
underlying the poetry of almost every writer included. In many
of the events described in the poems (bombings in Saigon,
for example, or the Hungarian uprisings), the Japanese are
merely spectators in a larger world of horror; this passive role
unfortunately imparts to the less-controlled poems a strident
tone that seems the poetic equivalent of hand-wringing.
Nevertheless, the issues are frighteningly real, and the poets
are passionately involved in them.

So is the Japanese editor, Kijima Hajime. His introduction
itself is a kind of poem, an impassioned statement on the "ashes,
vacuum, and 'given democracy' " that for him is the reality
in Japan today. What he has written is fascinating, but regretta-
bly he does not discuss the more factual aspects that would
be extremely helpful to a foreign reader: which Japanese poets
tend to work in groups, for example, or what the relation might
be between modern poetry and Western education. Many of
the poets are students and translators of Western literature,
yet the professional enthusiasm of none seems to extend to
Japanese or Chinese literature (either traditional or Marxist/
modern). References to a number of poetry prizes are made,
but no explanation on their sociological or artistic significance
is given. However, the anthology is a laudable effort of major
importance.

126. Kōno Ichiro, and Fukuda Rikutaro. *An Anthology of Modern Japanese Poetry*. Tokyo: Kenkyusha, 1957. xl, 173 pp.

This volume of translations, along with Enright and Ninomiya's *The Poetry of Living Japan* (no. **129**), both published in 1957, was one of the first anthologies on modern Japanese poetry, and it remains one of the best. A hundred poets are represented, far too many for such a brief volume, but the choices are well made. Both editors are respected poets in their own right, and their taste is catholic enough to include proletarian poetry and the work of a number of fairly obscure writers. Their introduction is brief but filled with quotations of poems, statements, parts of manifestos, and other documents that render the whole movement towards modern poetry in Japan quite vivid. The translations are accurately done, in English that is sensible and unobtrusive—perhaps a little too much so, in fact. Brief biographical sketches of the poets are included as an appendix.

On the whole there are few duplications with the translations provided in *The Poetry of Living Japan*; read together, the two books give a good picture of major poets and major trends since the turn of the century.

127. *The Literary Review*. Japan Number, vol. 6, no. 1 (Autumn 1962). 144 pp.

This issue is entirely devoted to postwar Japanese literature. Eleven contemporary poets are represented by a considerable number of translations, all prepared specifically for this publication by Ueda Makoto and others. Each poet has only a few poems to introduce him, but in the field of modern poetry, the reader is pleased to find what he can. Recommended. (*The Literary Review* is published at Fairleigh Dickenson University, Teaneck, New Jersey.)

128. *Literature East and West*. Vol. 13, nos. 3–4 (Dec., 1969): 404–428.

This issue contains translations of several poems each by three leading modern poets: Tamura Ryūichi, Takahashi Shinkichi (cf. no. **120**), and Hagiwara Sakutarō (cf. no. **114**). All three have been well translated in other volumes, but there are a number of poems that are not available elsewhere. For those interested in seeing the original Japanese texts, some samples are included.

Literature East and West, incidentally, is the most accessible forum in the United States for articles and book reviews on Asian literature and will continue to be of constant intérest to those looking for information on Japanese poetry. (Subscriptions are available for the journal at Box 8107, University Station, Austin, Texas 78712.)

129. Ninomiya Takamichi, and Enright, D.J. *The Poetry of Living Japan*. London: John Murray, 1957. 104 pp.

The development of new poetic forms in Japan that for many serious writers supplanted the traditional *haiku* and *waka* was a complex one that occupied Japanese poets until the 1920s, when Hagiwara Sakutarō (no. **114**) first gave a distinctive stamp to the modern Japanese poetic language. The precise nature of these experiments and adventures is difficult to render in translation, but Mr. Ninomiya, a distinguished Japanese scholar of English literature, and D.J. Enright, an excellent poet in his own right, have managed to provide in a short space several poems each by thirty important authors. Most of the finest poets are represented, even if briefly, beginning with Shimazaki Tōson, whose early attempts at writing in a romantic style at the turn of the century were highly influential, and ending with the writers active in the early postwar period. The translations are always musical and clear, and the choice of poems, while reflecting the individual tastes of the two translators, are sufficiently representative. Brief biographical sketches of the poets are included at the end of the book.

Needless to say, a work of this scope cannot hope to give the reader a sense of the nature of the work of any one poet; nevertheless, this early attempt to bring Japanese modern poetry to the attention of Western readers has not been superseded, despite its necessary shortcomings.

130. Sato Hiroaki, ed. *Ten Japanese Poets*. Paperbound. Hanover, New Hampshire: Granite Publications, 1973. 136 pp.

131. ————, ed. *Anthology of Modern Japanese Poets*. Paperbound. *Chicago Review* 25, no. 2 (1973). 146 pp.

Read together, these two anthologies, through the medium of Sato's vibrant and flexible English, stand the best chance of any work available to excite a reader, who is already conversant with sophisticated American and European poetry, with a contemporary Japanese view of what constitutes excellence in modern Japanese poetry.

The two books complement each other. Both contain prewar and postwar poets, and in several cases, the same poet appears in both, although no poems are duplicated. Traditionally respected poets such as Miyazawa Kenji and Hagiwara Sakutarō are included, and Sato's fine translations bring to their work a vitality heretofore missing. For example, this is Hagiwara's poem "The Swimmer" as rendered in the Shiffert/Sawa anthology (no. **133**):

> The swimmer's body stretches out slanting,
> two arms reach out together lengthily,
> the swimmer's heart is transparent like a jellyfish,
> the swimmer's eyes are hearing the sound of
>   suspended bells,
> the swimmer's spirit watches the moon over the water.
>   [Shiffert and Sawa, *Anthology of*
>   *Modern Japanese Poetry*, p. 48]

This is fine as a general paraphrase; Sato's version, however, moves with the inevitability of a poem in English:

> The swimmer's body expands aslant
> His arms, laid side by side, elongate
> The swimmer's heart is translucent like the jellyfish
> The swimmer's eyes hear the toll of the bell
> The swimmer's soul looks at the moon
>   [*Ten Japanese Poets*, p. 76]

Here are a few lines from the opening of a long poem, "End of Summer," by Takahashi Mutsuo, taken from *New Writing in Japan* (no. **121**).

> Raindrops thrash the windowpanes of night
> Right outside the window young trees tussle with each other
> Summer has ended
> O Abel frenzied summer is gone
> [Tr. by James Kirkup and Miura Fumiko, p. 234]

A fine enough beginning, yet for this reader at least, Sato has caught and pointed up the tortured urgency that sets the basic rhythms of the poem; if his English is less decorous, the energy quotient is higher.

> Raindrops beat night windowpanes
> Crowding the window, young trees torment each other
> The summer has ended
> Abel, I say the frenzied summer has gone
> [Ten Japanese Poets, p. 123]

Sato has also had the courage to translate poems that the other anthologists shy away from because of their difficulty. As a result, we now have very adequate versions of long poems by Nishiwaki Junzaburō, the famous "Chieko" poems written by Takamura Kōtarō about his wife who went insane, and poems on French art by Takiguchi Shūzō. Some readers may feel that Sato's diction is too colloquial here, but the general tone always seems correct.

Those wishing a sample of the humor, humanity, and intellectual vitality typical of the best in contemporary Japanese poetry would do well to read Sato's "Mutsuo Takahashi puts 76 Questions to Minoru Yoshioka" in the *Chicago Review* issue.

As a concluding example of Sato's accomplishments, here are three versions of the same short poem by Tamura Ryūichi. Those who value energy and conciseness, as well as accuracy, will find their choice easy to make. The fact that all three sound somewhat different will serve to remind the English-language reader how elusive a language Japanese can be.

> My suffering
> is plain
> > Like keeping an animal from a far-off land
> > There's no real need for a groom
>
> My poetry
> Is plain
> > Like reading a letter from a far-off land
> > There's no real need for tears

My joys and sorrows
Are still more plain
    Like killing a man from a far-off land
    There's no real need for words
        [Bownas, *New Writing in Japan*, p. 205]

You have to take a lot of trouble
looking after an animal from a far country

    My torments
    are simpler matters

You have to shed a lot of tears
when you receive a letter from a far country

    My poems
    are simpler things

You have to use a lot of words
to insult someone from a far country

    My joys and sorrows
    are simpler things
  [Guest and Kajima, *Post-War Japanese Poetry*, p. 90]

My sufferings are simple
    They require no such skills
    As does breeding animals from a distant country

My poems are simple
    They require no such tears
    As does reading a letter from a distant country

My joys and sorrows are simpler
    They require no such words
    As does killing a person from a distant country
      [Sato, *Anthology of Modern Japanese Poets*, p. 127]

There is little that is genteel in Sato's two volumes; some things may even be shocking, but there is not a line that can be taken for granted, and there may be no higher praise than that.

For those interested in exploring more of Sato's work, there are eleven poems by nine modern poets in the journal *Works* (vol. 4, no. 1, summer 1973), as well as additional translations in most issues of the fine poetry journal *Granite*, published since 1971 in Hanover, New Hampshire.

132. Sato Satoru, and Urdang, Constance, eds. "Contemporary Poetry in Japan." *Poetry,* no. 88 (May 1956). 124 pp.

The entire issue of the magazine is devoted to translations of twenty-seven modern Japanese poets ("contemporary" is hardly the word for the works of Shimazaki Tōson included here, which were written at the turn of the century). It serves as a small and well-prepared anthology, with a high proportion of selections that illustrate the editors' contention: "the aesthetic dilemma of modern poetry, the fact that art and beauty are not necessarily identical, seems more agonizing for the modern poet in Japan than for other poets."

Well worth looking up, the issue deserves a reprinting in book form.

133. Shiffert, Edith, and Sawa Yūki. *Anthology of Modern Japanese Poetry*. Rutland, Vermont, and Tokyo: Charles E. Tuttle Co., 1972. 195 pp.

This anthology of modern poetry, which includes free verse, *waka*, and *haiku*, covers much the same ground as the Enright/Ninomiya (no. **129**) and Kōno/Fukuda (no. **126**) volumes, with the addition of a certain amount of poetry written since the publication of those earlier volumes. The new translations in the present collection do not represent any improvement over earlier versions; in fact, although the translators have been quite free in their rendering of many of the texts, the English versions seldom exhibit any distinctive tone of their own. The biographical sketches at the end of the book are superior to those found elsewhere, but on the whole, the anthology makes no significant contribution.

134. Shimer, Dorothy Blair. *Voices of Modern Asia: An Anthology of Twentieth-century Asian Literature*. Paperbound. New York: New American Library, 1973. 376 pp.

For those wishing a modest introduction to twentieth-century Japanese poetry, this pleasant collection (in the fifteen pages allotted) will serve to illustrate some of the best known and respected modern Japanese poets, writing both in traditional forms and in free verse. The translations are chosen from those published in a variety of places by such fine translators as Donald Keene, D. J. Enright, Graeme Wilson, and Harold Wright.

135. Wilson, Graeme, and Atsumi Ikuko. *Three Contemporary Japanese Poets*. London: London Magazine Editions, 1972. 80 pp.

This is one of the best books available on contemporary Japanese poetry, precisely because the editors have concentrated on three important figures: Anzai Hitoshi, Shiraishi Kazuko, and Tanikawa Shuntarō. All three are represented in most of the other anthologies, but with only two or three poems by each. Here, with a number of poems to read and ponder over, the reader can begin to form a sense of their work.

The translations of each poet are preceded by informative, somewhat informal, essays on the writer's major artistic preoccupations. The editors attribute Anzai's unique style, reflected in such poems as "Hitomaro" or "Saigyō," to the poet's understanding of European poetry combined with his strong sense of Japanese tradition. Shiraishi is characterized as the contemporary "successor in erotic urgency" to two women poets, Ono no Komachi of the Heian period and Yosano Akiko (see no. **109**), who wrote at the beginning of this century. Born in Canada, Shiraishi mixes Japanese and American idioms in poems proclaiming a mordant, unflinching vitality. Tanikawa, considered by many to be the greatest general talent in poetry since the end of the war, exhibits an energy and a consuming interest in almost all facets of the world around him that makes it probable, as the introduction to his work suggests, that, "young as he still is, he has not yet written his best."

The translations have considerable tone and stand up with appropriate panache in their new language. Altogether, the book is quite a credible accomplishment.

136. The Japan Society, Inc. *Three Japanese Poets*. New York: The Japan Society, 1972. (Phonograph recording with texts and notes included.)

This fascinating and enjoyable recording was made at the Guggenheim Museum in New York on March 16, 1971, when three well known contemporary poets, Tamura Ryūichi, Tanikawa Shuntarō, and Katagiri Yūzuru, read in Japanese from their own works, at the invitation of the American Academy of Poets. A translation is read with each poem, so the voices of Gary Synder, the famous poet, and Harold Wright, the well-known critic and translator, can be heard as well.

Three Japanese Poets represents, at this writing, the only available recording of modern Japanese poetry.

(Copies of the recording can be purchased through the Japan Society, 333 East 47th Street, New York, N.Y. 10017.)

General Studies

137. Okazaki Yoshie. *Japanese Literature in the Meiji Era*. Tr. by V.H. Viglielmo. Japanese Culture in the Meiji Era, vol. 1. Tokyo: Toyo Bunko, 1955. xiv, 673 pp.

This large volume traces the literary developments in Japan from the 1860s to roughly the time of World War I, indicating the influences of foreign literature, the development of new artistic forms, and the changes brought about during that time in the traditional literary arts.

Three sections of the book are of special interest to readers of Japanese poetry: the discussion of the development of the so-called "new style" poetry, based on Western models, and the chapters on the reforms to *waka* and *haiku*.

The book is a good source of information on these subjects, perhaps the best available in English, but it is not well organized. The author's arguments are often lost in a maze of details; the text contains a good many repetitions, and the enormous number of names and miscellaneous facts may confound the reader. The volume was, of course, originally intended for readers who had the basic background necessary for a full comprehension of the subjects treated. For such readers, Okazaki's study is a valuable reference book.

138. Sugiyama Yoko. *"The Wasteland* and Contemporary Japa-
nese Poetry." *Comparative Literature* 13, no. 3 (Summer
1961): 264–78.

Early postwar poetry written in Japan, which was dominated
by images of destruction, Hiroshima, and the gloom of Eliot,
is the topic of this study. The author provides translations of
poems by Miyoshi Toyoichirō, Nakagiri Masao, and Ayukawa
Nobuo. The study is not profound, but at least it provides a
tenable introduction to the subject.

139. Yamagiwa, Joseph K. *Japanese Literature of the Shōwa
Period: A Guide to Japanese Reference and Research Materials.*
Paperbound. Ann Arbor: University of Michigan Press,
1959. xii, 212 pp.

The student of modern Japanese poetry is often—and right-
ly—troubled by the bewildering quantity of information he must
come to terms with—styles, schools, authors, manifestos, critics,
and all other aspects of a poetic tradition every bit as complex
and lively as those of America, France, or England.

Mr. Yamagiwa provides a map of the territory to guide the
reader in his studies: all genres of literature are covered, of
course, but his sections on poetry deal with "new style" poetry,
waka, and *haiku* and include discussions on styles, authors,
poetry groups, magazines, and various other pertinent aspects
of the subject. There is also a useful annotated bibliography
of basic reference works in Japanese, as well as a list of important
works by each author mentioned.

The book is intended mainly for those who can read Japanese,
but Yamagiwa's information is clearly presented and accessible
to any reader. Unfortunately, by limiting his research to the
Shōwa period (1926 to the present), the author perforce finds
many of his important authors and movements already, as it
were, in mid-career. Some information is provided on prior
developments, but a corresponding volume on the Taishō period
(1912–26) would be helpful.

INDEX

Authors, editors, translators, and titles given in each numbered entry are presented below. In addition, Japanese authors and works of literature mentioned in the body of the annotations and in the General Introduction and the Historical Sketch and Bibliographic Outline are indexed as an aid to the reader in finding more complete references. The personal name by which a writer may be commonly known is followed by the family name in parenthesis. Italicized page numbers indicate major references to annotated items.